EAT GREEN, GET LEAN

100 VEGETARIAN AND VEGAN RECIPES FOR BUILDING MUSCLE, GETTING LEAN, AND STAYING HEALTHY

Michael Matthews

oculus

ISBN-978-1-938895-21-0

Cover Designed by: Damon Freeman

Typesetting by Kiersten Lief

Published by: Waterbury Publishers, Inc.

www.oculuspublishers.com

Visit the author's website:

www.muscleforlife.com

ABOUT THE AUTHOR

Hi,

I'm Mike and I've been training for nearly a decade now.

I believe that every person can achieve the body of his or her dreams, and I work hard to give everyone that chance by providing workable, proven advice grounded in science, not a desire to sell phony magazines, workout products, or supplements.

Through my work, I've helped thousands of people achieve their health and fitness goals, and I share everything I know in my books.

So if you're looking to get in shape and look great, then I think I can help you. I hope you enjoy my books and I'd love to hear from you at my site, www.muscleforlife.com.

Sincerely,

Mike

CONTENTS

Adding some addition flavor to a meal can mean the difference between good and great.

In this section, you'll find the following recipes:

SNACKS   157

One of the biggest problems for people dieting is the constant snacking or "grazing." Learn how to make some healthy snacks to curb your appetite without sacrificing diet.

In this section, you'll find the following recipes:

Snack Recipes for Vegetarians   159

Trying to get protein every 3 hours can be tough. This is where shakes come in.

In this section, you'll find the following recipes:

Eating healthy doesn't mean never having dessert, and you don't have to be an expert baker to make these dishes.

In this section, you'll find the following recipes:

Chances are you'd like to use the recipes in this book to plan out your meals. This handy spreadsheet will help! In it you'll find a list of every recipe in the book along with their calories, protein, carbs, and fats!

BUILD MUSCLE AS A VEGETARIAN OR VEGAN

MORE AND MORE PEOPLE ARE turning to vegetarian and vegan lifestyles for moral reasons or their many health benefits, or both. Many athletes are wary to make the jump, however, because they believe it's not possible to build a strong, muscular body if you don't eat meats and animal products. They're wrong.

The reality is you can make fantastic gains with exercise, weightlifting included, as a vegetarian or vegan if you know what you're doing, which is the reality for meat-eaters, too (just because you work out and eat a bunch of animal protein every day doesn't mean you're going to get stronger or more muscular).

Another problem that most people share, regardless of their dietary preferences, is the fact that eating properly to build muscle or lose fat presents unique problems if you're not good in the kitchen.

Eating to build muscle requires that you eat quite a bit of food each day, and forcing down large quantities of bland proteins and grains, legumes, and tubers day after day gets really old, really fast. And running amok and eating everything your stomach desires is a sure route to packing on an ever-expanding layer of unnecessary fat.

On the other hand, eating to lose fat requires that you carefully watch your food intake to maintain a caloric deficit each day (that you eat less potential energy—calories—than you burn through basic bodily functions and activity). This leaves no room for the fatty and sweet indulgences that so many people crave, and it's only a matter of time until you can't look at another pile of steamed veggies.

The good news is there's a simple solution to the above problems. By learning how to cook fast, healthy, and tasty meals that provide adequate protein, carbs, and fats, you can enjoy eating to build muscle or lose fat. And following a vegetarian or vegan diet won't get in your way.

That's what this book is all about.

In it, you're going to find a compilation of my favorite vegetarian and vegan recipes that fit the bill. Every recipe in this book is designed to help you build lean muscle or lose fat while actually getting healthier (because who cares if you look great but feel like crap?). And they all TASTE GOOD.

So why buy this book?

Because following a diet, whether to get more muscular or lose fat, is SO much more pleasurable when you can enjoy your meals. I think this book will become a good friend.

WHAT MAKES
EAT GREEN, GET LEAN
DIFFERENT?

AS YOU PROBABLY KNOW, you must eat properly to see good results from working out. You can grind away on the treadmill and pound weights until the cows come home and still see little to no results if you don't know how to support those activities with the right nutrition.

Muscles can't grow unless the body has the right nutrients to repair the damage caused by lifting weights. Eat too little, and you can not only fail to make gains, but you can actually lose muscle.

Your body can't lose fat unless you make it operate at just the right deficit of calories. Eat just a few hundred too many calories per day, and you'll find yourself stuck in the miserable rut of feeling like you're "on a diet" without losing any weight.

That being said, many diet plans out there exist in a vacuum. That is, they assume that eating conditions will always remain the same. They don't take into account the fact that most people can't stomach the same handful of food options every day, or that being severely restricted in one's diet can lead to all-out splurging, which then leads to the dreaded weight yo-yo.

What's needed is balance—a diet that allows for a variety of foods and that allows you to indulge now and again. It also has to be simple and practical so as to fit in with the craziness of our daily lives. And last but not least, it needs to enhance your overall health by incorporating healthy proteins, carbs, and fats instead of the junk found in most people's fridges.

Well, that's what Eat Green Get Lean is all about. If you follow the advice given in this book, you'll not only find it easy to follow diets to gain muscle or lose fat, but you'll also be able to actually enjoy them.

As you'll see, most of the recipes are sorted into two categories: recipes for getting big and recipes for getting lean.

Recipes for getting big are going to be higher-calorie meals with a fair amount of carbs and fats, and they'll help you reach your daily calorie needs for building muscle.

Recipes for getting lean are lower-calorie meals with little carbs and fats, which is vital for dieting successfully.

HOW TO EAT RIGHT
WITHOUT OBSESSING OVER
EVERY CALORIE

I HAVE GOOD NEWS.

You can look and feel great without breaking out a calculator every time you eat.

Getting proper nutrition is a precise science, but it doesn't have to be agonizing. In fact, I recommend a more laid-back approach. If you make planning or tracking meals too complicated, you'll have trouble sticking with it.

That being said, in order to lose fat, you must keep your body burning more energy than you're feeding it, and the energy potential of food is measured in calories. Eat too many calories—give your body more potential energy than it needs—and it has no incentive to burn fat.

In order to gain muscle, your body needs a surplus of energy to repair and rebuild itself (along with plenty of protein). Thus, you need to eat slightly more than your body burns to get bigger.

In this chapter I'm going to share some simple rules that you can follow to eat right. Just by following these rules, you'll find that you can lose or gain weight when you want to and that you'll feel healthy and vital.

1. MAKE SURE YOU EAT ENOUGH

A calorie is a measurement of the potential energy found in food, and your body burns quite a bit of energy every day. Everything from the beating of your heart to the digestion of your food requires energy, and your body has to get it from the food you eat.

Thus, it's important that you feed your body enough, and that's especially true when you work out. If you underfeed your body, don't be surprised if you don't have the energy to train hard or if you feel generally exhausted.

If you exercise at least three times per week, use the following formula to ensure you're feeding your body enough to repair itself.

- Eat 1 gram of protein per pound of body weight per day. = 120g
- Eat 1.5 grams of carbs per pound of body weight per day. = 180g
- Eat 1 gram of healthy fats per 4 pounds of body weight per day. 30g

That's where you start. For a 130 lb. woman, it would look like this:

- 130 grams of protein per day
- 195 grams of carbs per day
- 32 grams of fat per day

That's about 1,600 calories per day, which should work for making slow, steady muscle and strength gains without any fat added along the way (which really should be the goal of "maintenance"—not staying exactly the same).

The above targets are fairly easy for a vegetarian to meet as she has plenty of plant-based proteins to choose from as well as lean protein sources like egg whites and low-fat dairy products. It gets trickier for vegans, however, because their best sources of protein also come with a considerable amount of carbs and fats.

Therefore, I recommend vegans rely on soy products such as tofu (lite and extra-lite are best) and tempeh, grains (quinoa and amaranth are probably the most popular) and legumes (with all types of beans being the most popular choice here). Supplementing with vegan protein powders, which are usually blends of proteins from rice, hemp, peas, and other sources, also makes balancing your numbers easier.

If your priority is to gain muscle, then you need to add about 500 calories per day to your "maintenance" diet. The easiest way to do this is to bump up your carbs by about 50 grams per day, and your fats by about 30 grams per day.

If you're trying to lose fat, then you need to subtract about 500 calories per day from your maintenance diet. To do this, drop your carbs by about 90 grams per day, your protein by about 10 grams per day.

It's also important that you consume high-quality calories. Junk food calories, such as white bread and pastas, chips, and juice and soda, will make you look and feel like crap, while good calories, such as fruits, vegetables, whole grains, and high-quality proteins, will keep you in tip-top shape.

2. EAT ENOUGH HIGH QUALITY PROTEIN

If you work out, you need more protein than someone who doesn't work out. Why? Because exercise causes muscle damage, and protein is used to repair this damage.

With every rep you perform, you're causing "micro-tears" in your muscle fibers, and your body uses amino acids—what proteins are made up of—to repair them. The body doesn't just repair them to their previous state, however; it builds them bigger and stronger so it can better handle the stress of exercise.

So, in order to get the most out of your workouts, you need to eat enough high-quality protein. And that doesn't mean just eating a lot after working out. It means having protein 4 – 6 times per day with a few hours in between each meal.

By doing this, you can keep your body in an "anabolic" state, which means a state in which it is building muscle and repairing tissue. If you fail to feed your body enough protein each day, it will fall behind in the muscle breakdown and repair cycle, and your body will go into a "catabolic" state, meaning that it will actually break down muscle and other tissue despite exercise.

There are two main sources of protein out there: whole food protein and supplement protein.

Whole food protein is, as you guessed, protein that comes from natural food sources, such as eggs, cottage cheese, and quinoa. The best forms of whole food protein that you will want to choose from are quinoa, low-fat Greek yogurt, tempeh, tofu, eggs, almonds, rice, and beans.

Now, some people claim that you must carefully combine your proteins if you're vegetarian or vegan to ensure your body is getting "complete" proteins (all of the amino acids needed to build tissue). This theory and the faulty research it was based on was thoroughly debunked as a myth by the American Dietetic Association, yet it still hangs around. While it's true that some sources of vegetable protein are lower in certain amino acids than other forms of protein, there is no scientific evidence to prove that they lack them altogether.

Protein supplements are powdered or liquid foods that contain protein from various sources, such as whey (a liquid remaining after milk has been curdled and strained in the process of making cheese), egg, and soy—the three most common sources of supplement protein. There are also great plant-based supplements out there that are a blend of high-quality protein sources such as quinoa, brown rice, peas, hemp, and fruit.

You don't NEED protein supplements to eat well, but it can be impractical for some to try to get all protein from whole foods considering the fact that you will be eating protein 4 – 6 times per day.

Now, there are a few things you should know about eating protein. First is the subject of how much protein you can absorb in one sitting. Studies relating to this are very contradictory and disputed, mainly because it's a complex subject. Your genetics, metabolism, digestive tract health, lifestyle, and amount of lean mass are all important factors. But in the spirit of keeping things simple, here's what we know: you can eat and properly use a lot of protein in each meal. How much, exactly? Well, your body should have no trouble absorbing upwards of 100 grams in one sitting.

That said, there aren't any benefits of eating this way (I find gorging quite uncomfortable, actually), but it's good to know in case you miss a meal and need to make it up by loading protein into a later meal.

Another thing to know about protein is that different proteins digest at different speeds, and some are better utilized by the body than others. Whey protein is digested quickly and its "net protein utilization" (NPU) is in the low 90% range, meaning that your body can absorb and use 90%+ of what you eat. Egg protein digests much more slowly than whey, but its NPU falls in the same range.

NPU and digestion speeds are important to know because you want to rely on high-NPU proteins to meet your daily protein requirement, and you want a quick-digesting protein for your post-workout meal, and a slow-digesting protein for your final meal before you go to bed (to help you get through the overnight fast).

I could give you charts and tables of the NPU rates of various proteins, but I'm going to just keep it simple. In order to meet your daily protein requirements, here are your choices:

Whole Food Proteins

Eggs

Quinoa

Brown Rice

Amaranth

Dairy

Tempeh

Tofu

Beans

Almonds

Protein Supplements

Egg

Whey

Casein

Rice or other vegan proteins

3. EAT HEALTHY FATS

Fats are the densest energy source available to your body. Each gram of fat contains over twice the calories of a gram of carbohydrate or protein. Healthy fats, such as those found in olive oil, avocados, flax seed oil, many nuts, and other foods, are actually an important component for overall good health. Fats help your body absorb the other nutrients that you give it, they nourish the nervous system, help maintain cell structures, regulate hormone levels, and more.

Certain fats are unhealthy, though, and can lead to disease and other health problems. These types of fats are called trans fats.

Trans fats are scientifically modified saturated fats that have been engineered to give foods longer shelf lives. Many cheap, packaged foods are full of trans fats (such as run-of-the-mill popcorn, yogurt, and peanut butter) as are many frozen foods (such as frozen pizza, packaged pastries, cakes, etc.). And fried foods are often fried in trans fats. These fats are bad news, and eating too much of them can lead to all kinds of diseases and complications. They have no nutritional value for the body and thus should be avoided altogether.

Most people eat more fat than is necessary, thus adding lots of unnecessary calories to their daily intake. Getting enough healthy fats every day is pretty simple. Here's how it works:

- Keep your intake of saturated fats low (below 10% of your total calories). Saturated fat is found in foods like meat, dairy products, eggs, coconut oil, and lard. If a fat is solid at room temperature, it's a saturated fat.

- Completely avoid trans fats, which are the worst type of saturated fat. Trans fats are found in processed foods such as cookies, cakes, fries, and donuts. Any food that contains "hydrogenated oil" or "partially hydrogenated oil" likely contains trans fats, so just don't eat it. (Sure, having a cheat here and there that contains trans fats won't harm anything, but you definitely don't want to eat them regularly.)

- Get most of your fat from unsaturated fats such as olive oil, nuts, peanut oil, avocados, flax seed oil, safflower oil, sesame oil, or cottonseed oil. If a fat is liquid at room temperature, it's an unsaturated fat.

By simply sticking to the recipes in this book, you'll avoid unhealthy fats and eat healthy fats without even trying.

4. EAT GOOD CARBS

The carbohydrate is probably the most misunderstood, maligned, and feared macro-nutrient. Thanks to the scores of bogus diet plans and suggestions out there, many people equate eating carbs with getting fat. While eating TOO MANY carbs can make you fat (just as eating too much protein or fat can), carbs are hardly your enemy. They play an essential role in not only muscle growth but in overall body function.

Regardless of what type of carbohydrate you eat—broccoli or apple pie—the body breaks it down into two substances: glucose and glycogen. Glucose is commonly referred to as "blood sugar," and it's an energy source used by your cells to do the many things they do. Glycogen is a substance stored in the liver and muscles that can be easily converted to glucose for immediate energy. When you lift weights intensely, your muscles burn up their glycogen stores to cope with the overload.

Now, why is broccoli good for you but apple pie isn't? Because your body reacts very differently to broccoli than to apple pie. You've probably heard the terms "simple" and "complex" carbs before and wondered what they meant. You might have also heard of the glycemic index and wondered what it was all about.

These things are actually pretty simple. The glycemic index is a numeric system of ranking how quickly carbohydrates are converted into glucose in the body. Carbs are ranked on a scale of 0 to 100 depending how they affect blood sugar levels once eaten. A GI rating of 55 and under is considered "low GI," 56 to 69 is medium, and 70 and above is high on the index. A "simple" carb is one that converts very quickly (is high on the glycemic index), such as table sugar, honey, and watermelon, while a "complex" carb is one that converts slowly (is low on the glycemic index), such as broccoli, apple, and whole-grain bread.

It's very important to know where the carbs you eat fall on the index, because studies have linked regular consumption of high-GI carbs to increased risk for heart disease, diabetes, and obesity.

The amount of carbohydrates that you should eat every day depends on what you're trying to accomplish. Building muscle requires that you eat a substantial amount of carbs, while dieting to lose weight requires that you reduce carbs.

Regardless of how many carbs you need to eat per day, there's a simple rule to follow regarding high-, medium- and low-glycemic carbs.

Eat carbs in the medium–high range of the glycemic index (70 – 90 is a good rule of thumb) about 30 minutes before you exercise, and again within 30 minutes of finishing your workout.

The reason you want some carbs before training is that you need the energy for it. The reason you want them after is that your muscles' glycogen stores are heavily depleted, and by replacing it quickly, you actually help your body repair the damage and maintain an anabolic state.

My favorite pre- and post-workout carbs are bananas and rice milk, but other good choices are sweet potato, instant oatmeal, and fruits that are above 60 on the glycemic index, such as cantaloupe, pineapple, watermelon, dates, apricots, and figs. Some people recommend eating foods high in table sugar (sucrose) after working out because it's high on the GI, but I stay away from processed sugar as much as possible.

All other carbs you eat should be in the middle or at the low end of the glycemic index (60 and below is a good rule of thumb). It really is that simple. If you follow this rule, you'll avoid many problems that others suffer from due to the energy highs and lows that come with eating high-GI carbs that burn the body out.

Below are some examples of tasty, healthy carbs that you can include in your diet.

FOOD	GI
Oatmeal	58
Brown rice	55

Whole grain sourdough bread	48
Multi-grain muffin	45
Multi-grain bread	43
Basmati rice	43
Orange	42
Strawberries	40
Apple	38
Yam	37
Blackberries	32
Black beans	30
Peanuts	14
Almonds	10

So, forget stuff like sugar, white bread, processed, low-quality whole wheat bread, bagels, junk cereals, muffins, white pasta, crackers, waffles, rice cakes, corn flakes, and white rice. I wouldn't even recommend eating these things often as pre- or post-workout carbs because they're just not good for your body.

Even certain fruits, such as watermelon and dates, are bad snack foods because of where they fall on the glycemic index. If you're unsure about a carb you like, look it up to see where it falls on the glycemic index. If it's above 60, just leave it out of your meals that aren't immediately before or after working out.

5. EAT PLENTY OF FRUITS AND VEGGIES

Your body requires many different things to function optimally. It can't look and feel great on protein and carbs alone. You need calcium to ensure your muscles can contract and relax properly. You need fiber to help move food through the digestive tract. You need iron to carry oxygen to your cells and create energy.

There are many other "little helpers" that your body needs to perform its many physiological processes, and fruits and vegetables contain many vital nutrients that you can't get from vitamin supplements. By eating 3 – 5 servings of both fruits and vegetables per day, you enjoy the many benefits that these nutrients give to your body, such as lowering your risk of cancer, heart disease, diabetes, and many other diseases.

This isn't hard to do, either. A medium-sized piece of fruit is one serving, as is half a cup of berries. A cup of greens is a serving of vegetables, as is half a cup of other vegetables.

Store-bought fruit juices, however, are another story. While they may seem like an easy way to get in your daily fruits, they are actually not much more than tasty sugar water. Not only do most fruit juices have sugar added, but the juice has also been separated from the fruit's fibrous pulp, which slows down the metabolism of the sugars. Without that, the juice becomes a very high-glycemic drink. You're better off drinking water and eating whole fruit.

The exception to this is creating juice using a juicer or blender to grind up the entire piece of fruit, removing nothing. This, of course, is no different than chewing up the fruit in your mouth.

Fruits widely recognized as the healthiest are apples, bananas, blueberries, oranges, grapefruit, strawberries, and pineapples.

Vegetables often recommended as the healthiest are asparagus, broccoli, spinach, sweet potatoes, tomatoes, carrots, onions, and eggplant.

6. PLAN AND PROPORTION YOUR MEALS PROPERLY

Many people's meal plans are engineered for getting fat. They skip breakfast, eat a junk food lunch, come home famished, have a big dinner with some dessert, and then have a snack like chips or popcorn while watching TV at night.

A much better strategy is to eat smaller meals every 3 – 4 hours, and include protein with each (as this fills you up and makes you feel satisfied).

Much of your daily carbohydrates should come before and after training, when your body needs them most. I eat about 10 – 15% of my daily carbs before training, and about 30 – 40% after, in my post-workout meal.

It's also important when dieting to lose weight to not eat carbs within several hours of going to bed. This advice has been kicking around the health and fitness world for quite some time, but usually with the wrong explanation.

There's no scientific evidence that eating carbs at night or before bed will lead to gaining fat, but it can hinder fat loss. How?

The insulin created by the body to process and absorb carbs eaten stops the use of fat as an energy source. Your body naturally burns the most fat while sleeping, and so going to sleep with elevated insulin levels interferes with fat loss.

Related to this is the fact that studies have indicated that the production and processing of insulin interferes with the production and processing of growth hormone, which has powerful fat-burning properties. Your body naturally produces much of its growth hormone while sleeping, so again, if your body is flushed with insulin when you go to sleep, your growth hormone production may suffer, which in turn may rob you of its fat-burning and muscle-building benefits.

So, as a general rule, when you're dieting to lose weight, don't eat any carbs within 4 – 5 hours of bedtime. You should only consume lean proteins after dinner. I follow this rule when bulking too, not because I'm worried about fat burning (you don't burn fat when bulking), but because I don't want to stunt my growth hormone production.

You can spread your fats throughout the day. I like to start my day with 1 – 2 tablespoons of a 3-6-9 blend (a combination of essential fatty acids, which are fats vital for the proper function of every cell, tissue, gland, and organ in your body), but you don't have to get one if you don't want to. You can simply stick to the sources of healthy fat given earlier.

7. DRINK A LOT OF WATER

The human body is about 60% water in adult males and about 70% in adult females. Muscles are about 70% water. That alone tells you how important staying hydrated is to maintaining good health and proper body function. Your body's ability to digest, transport, and absorb nutrients from food is dependent upon proper fluid intake. Water helps prevent injuries in the gym by cushioning joints and other soft-tissue areas. When your body is dehydrated, literally every physiological process is negatively affected.

I really can't stress enough the importance of drinking clean, pure water. It has zero calories, so it will never cause you to gain weight regardless of how much you drink. (You can actually harm your body by drinking too much water, but this would require that you drink several gallons per day.)

The Institute of Medicine reported in 2004 that women should consume about 91 ounces of water—or three-quarters of a gallon—per day, and men should consume about 125 ounces per day (a gallon is 128 ounces).

Now, keep in mind that those numbers include the water found in food. The average person gets about 80% of their water from drinking it and other beverages, and about 20% from the food they eat.

I've been drinking 1 – 2 gallons of water per day for years now, which is more than the IOM baseline recommendation, but I sweat a fair amount due to exercise and I live in Florida, which surely makes my needs higher.

I fill a one-gallon jug at the start of my day and simply make sure that I finish it by dinner time. By the time I go to bed, I'll have drunk a few more glasses.

Make sure the water you drink is filtered, purified water and not tap water (disgusting, but some people drink it). There's a big difference between drinking clean, alkaline water that your body can fully utilize and drinking polluted, acidic junk from the tap or bottle (which is the case with certain brands such as Dasani and Aquafina).

8. CUT BACK ON THE SODIUM

The average American's diet is so over-saturated with sodium it makes my head spin.

The Institute of Medicine recommends 1,500 milligrams of sodium per day as the adequate intake level for most adults. According to the Center for Disease Control, the average American aged 2 and up eats 3,436 milligrams of sodium per day.

Too much sodium in the body causes water retention (which gives you that puffy, soft look) and it can lead to high blood pressure and heart disease.

Whenever possible, I chose low- or no-sodium ingredients for the recipes in this book. When you need to add salt, I recommend sea salt or Himalayan rock salt (sounds like fancy BS, but it's actually great stuff) because they have many naturally occurring minerals, whereas run-of-the-mill table salt has been "chemically cleaned" to remove "impurities," which includes these vital elements.

9. CHEAT CORRECTLY

Many people struggling with diets talk about "cheat days." The idea is that if you're good during the week, you can go buck wild on the weekends and somehow not gain fat. Well, unless you have a very fast metabolism, that's not how it works. If you follow a strict diet and exercise, you can expect to lose 1 – 2 pounds per week. If you get too crazy, you can gain it right back over a weekend.

So don't think cheat DAYS, think cheat MEALS—meals where you eat more or less anything you want (and all other meals of the week follow your meal plan). When done once or twice per week, a cheat meal is not only satisfying, but it can actually help you lose fat.

How?

Well, first there's the psychological boost, which keeps you happy and motivated, which ultimately makes sticking to your diet easier.

But there's also a physiological boost.

Studies on overfeeding (the scientific term for binging on food) show that doing so can boost your metabolic rate by anywhere from 3 – 10%. While this sounds good, it actually doesn't mean much when you consider that you would need to eat anywhere from a few hundred to a few thousand extra calories in a day to achieve this effect.

More important are the effects cheating has on a hormone called leptin, which regulates hunger, your metabolic rate, appetite, motivation, and libido, as well as serving other functions in your body.

When you're in a caloric deficit and lose body fat, your leptin levels drop. This, in turn, causes your metabolism to slow down, your appetite to increase, your motivation to wane, and your mood to sour.

On the other hand, when you give your body more energy (calories) than it needs, leptin levels are boosted, which can then have positive effects on fat oxidation, thyroid activity, mood, and even testosterone levels.

So if it's a leptin boost that you really want, how do you best achieve it?

Eating carbohydrates is the most effective way. Second to that is eating protein (high-protein meals also raise your metabolic rate). Dietary fats aren't very effective at increasing leptin levels, and alcohol actually inhibits it.

So, if your weight is stuck and you're irritable and demotivated, a nice kick of leptin might be all you need to get the scales moving again.

Have a nice cheat meal full of protein and carbs, and feel good about it.

(I would recommend, however, that you don't go too overboard with your cheat meals—don't eat 2,000 calories of junk food and desserts and think it won't do anything.)

How many cheat meals you should eat per week depends on what you're trying to accomplish.

When you're eating to stay lean and gain muscle slowly, two cheat meals per week is totally fine. When you're dieting to lose weight, you can have one cheat meal per week.

SUMMARY

You may find this chapter a bit hard to swallow (no pun intended). Some people have a really hard time giving up their unhealthy eating habits (sugar and junk food can be pretty addictive). That being said, consider the following benefits of following the advice in this chapter:

1. If this is a completely new way of eating for you, I *guarantee* you'll feel better than you have in a *long* time. You won't have energy highs and lows. You won't have energy highs and lows. You won't feel lethargic. You won't have that mental fogginess that comes with being stuffed full of unhealthy food every day.

2. You will appreciate "bad" food so much more when you only have it once or twice per week. You'd be surprised how much better a dessert tastes when you haven't had one in a week. (You may also be surprised that junk food that you loved in the past no longer tastes good.)

3. You will actually come to enjoy healthy foods. I *promise*. Even if they don't taste good to you at first, just groove in the routine, and soon you'll crave brown rice and fruit instead of doughnuts and bread. Your body will adapt.

This chapter teaches you all there really is to eating properly so you can build muscle or lose weight on demand, all while staying healthy.

LET'S GET COOKING

GETTING LEAN, WHILE STILL feeding your muscles and body what they need, can be tough. That's why I wrote this book, and I'm confident that you'll be able to find the right recipes to fit your needs.

Nothing in this book is fancy or hard to make, yet many of the recipes are quite delicious. I'm sure that you'll find some new staples for your diet in this book.

The most you'll need to make these recipes is a blender and a couple pots and pans (most don't even need the blender). The instructions are easy to follow, the prep times are minimal, and the ingredients are easy to find. Cooking doesn't get much simpler than this.

I recommend that you pick out a week's worth of recipes and then go shopping for the ingredients. Many of the recipes use the same ingredients, which will save you money and time.

So, let's get started!

BREAKFAST

ALTHOUGH THE BODY APPEARS to "shut down" during sleep, this is far from the truth. It's incredibly active while you sleep, repairing muscle and producing hormones.

If you slept eight hours and ate your last meal five hours before going to bed, your body has gone thirteen hours without food. If you were to wake up and skip breakfast, waiting another five hours for the noon lunch, the fasting period stretches to eighteen hours.

During the starvation period of sleep, your body goes into a catabolic state (breaking muscle down), and the longer you extend it, the worse the situation gets. You want to end this as soon as possible, and you do it by eating food.

So, make a little time each morning for a breakfast—even if it's only a few minutes. You can make some of the recipes in advance and keep them in the fridge. Or you can make quick meals like oatmeal or egg scrambles. And if you have a little time, and so desire, treat yourself to something like pancakes.

BREAKFAST RECIPES FOR VEGETARIANS

ORANGE RICOTTA PANCAKES

Servings: 6 (2 pancakes per serving)

Prep Time: 5 mins

Cooking Time: 10 mins

(Per Serving)

Calories: 242

Protein: 21 grams

Carbohydrates: 27 grams

Fat: 5 grams

1 cup barley flour

1/3 cup all-purpose flour

2 tablespoons stevia or other natural sweetener

3 scoops vanilla whey protein powder (available Tesco and Holland & Barratt)

2 teaspoons baking powder

1/2 teaspoon baking soda

1 cup fat free ricotta cheese

1/2 cup skimmed milk

1/2 cup orange juice

1 teaspoon orange zest

2 large eggs, beaten

1 tablespoon unsalted butter

1 teaspoon vanilla extract

> In a large mixing bowl, add the barley, flour, stevia, protein powder, baking powder, and baking soda and mix until well combined. Set aside.

> In a separate large mixing bowl, add the ricotta, skimmed milk, orange juice, orange zest, eggs, butter, and vanilla extract. Beat together until mixed well. Slowly mix liquid ingredients into dry ingredients until just mixed. Do not overmix.

> Coat a large non-stick skillet in cooking spray and wipe away the excess with a paper towel. Save this for wiping the pan after each pancake. Heat the skillet over medium heat.

> Spoon about 3 to 4 tablespoons of batter on to the griddle and cook until bubbles appear. Flip and cook until golden brown.

> Repeat step 4 with the remaining batter.

EGGS & QUINOA INSTANT BREAKFAST

Servings: 1

Prep Time: 1 min

Cooking Time: Under 5 mins

(Per Serving)

Calories: 286

Protein: 22 grams

Carbohydrates: 40 grams

Fat: 5 grams

4 egg whites

2/3 cup quinoa, cooked

1 tsp of maple syrup

1/3 cup almond milk (available from Asda and Holland & Barratt)

1/2 cup mixed berries

> Add the egg whites to a microwave-safe bowl. Cover with paper towel or lid and microwave for 2 – 3 minutes or until cooked.
> Add quinoa and almond milk to the bowl. Microwave for 1 minute. Top with maple syrup and berries.

PROTEIN OATCAKES

Servings: 2 (2 oatcakes per serving)

Prep Time: 3 mins

Cooking Time: 5 – 6 mins

(Per Serving)

Calories: 223

Protein: 31 grams

Carbohydrates: 20 grams

Fat: 2 grams

1/2 cup old-fashioned oats

1/2 cup fat-free cottage cheese

6 egg whites

1/2 teaspoon cinnamon

1/2 teaspoon vanilla extract

1/8 teaspoon baking powder

1 scoop vanilla whey protein powder (available Tesco and Holland & Barratt)

> Place all ingredients in a large mixing bowl and mix with a whisk or electric hand mixer until it thickens into a batter.

> Coat a large non-stick skillet in cooking spray and wipe away the excess with a paper towel. Save this for wiping the pan after cooking each pancake. Heat the skillet over medium heat.

> Pour or ladle about 1/2 cup of the batter on to the skillet and cook, 2 – 3 minutes each side until golden brown. Repeat for remaining batter.

HEALTHY FRENCH TOAST

Servings: 1

Prep Time: 2 mins

Cooking Time: 5 mins

(Per Serving)

Calories: 421

Protein: 38 grams

Carbohydrates: 60 grams

Fat: 4 grams

14 egg whites

1/4 cup skimmed milk

1/8 teaspoon cinnamon

1/2 scoop vanilla whey protein powder (available Tesco and Holland & Barratt)

2 slices whole grain bread

1 banana, sliced or 1 1/2 cups mixed berries

> In a medium-sized mixing bowl, add the egg whites, milk, cinnamon, and protein powder and whisk until thoroughly combined.
> Coat a large non-stick skillet in cooking spray and place over medium heat.

> Soak the bread in the egg white mixture for 10 – 15 seconds, then place in the skillet. Cook for 2 – 3 minutes, then flip. Pour the egg mixture in the pan around the bread and cook.

> Transfer to a plate then top with banana or berries.

"COOKIE DOUGH" OATMEAL CEREAL

Servings: 1

Prep Time: 3 – 4 mins

(Per Serving)

Calories: 496

Protein: 30 grams

Carbohydrates: 47 grams

Fat: 23 grams

1/2 cup old-fashioned oats

1/2 scoop vanilla whey protein powder (available Tesco and Holland & Barratt)

1/4 teaspoon cinnamon

1/4 teaspoon stevia or other natural sweetener

1/8 teaspoon vanilla extract

salt, to taste

2 tablespoons almond butter (available in Holland & Barratt)

1 cup skimmed milk

> In a medium-sized bowl, add the oats, protein powder, cinnamon, stevia, vanilla extract, and salt. Mix together well.

> Add the almond butter, one small chunk at a time. Stir into the mixture allowing it to break up slightly until it resembles crumbly cookie dough.

> Top with skimmed milk.

SPICY TEX-MEX BREAKFAST BURRITO

Servings: 1

Prep Time: 5 mins

Cooking Time: 5 mins

(Per Serving)

Calories: 294

Protein: 28 grams

Carbohydrates: 42 grams

Fat: 5 grams

1 (10 inch/25 cm) whole grain tortilla

1/2 teaspoon jalapeño, seeded and diced

2 tablespoons red bell pepper, diced

2 tablespoons green bell pepper, diced

2 tablespoons onion, diced

2 tablespoons tomato, diced

5 egg whites

1 tablespoon low-fat cheddar cheese, shredded

1 tablespoon fresh coriander, chopped

> Coat a medium-sized skillet in cooking spray and place over medium heat. Add the jalapeños, bell peppers, onion, and tomato. Sauté for 2 – 3 minutes, or until tender.

> Pour in the eggs and scramble. Once cooked, transfer egg mixture to a plate. Place the tortilla in the hot pan and warm, about 1 minute on each side. Remove tortilla from heat and top with egg mixture, sprinkle with cheese and coriander.

BLACK BEAN BREAKFAST BURRITO

Servings: 1

Prep Time: 2 mins

Cooking Time: 5 mins

(Per Serving)

Calories: 316

Protein: 23 grams

Carbohydrates: 52 grams

Fat: 7 grams

1 (10 inch/25 cm) whole grain tortilla

2 egg whites

1/4 cup black beans, drained and rinsed

2 tablespoons salsa

2 tablespoons low-fat cheddar cheese, shredded

1 tablespoon fat-free sour cream

> Coat a small non-stick skillet in cooking spray, add the eggs and scramble. After 1 – 2 minutes add the beans and cook until eggs are done and beans are heated. Remove egg mixture from pan and stir in salsa and cheese.

> Place the tortilla in the hot pan and cook until warm, about 1 minute each side. Remove tortilla from pan and top with egg mixture and sour cream.

ASIAN EGG SCRAMBLE

Servings: 1

Prep Time: 5 mins

Cooking Time: 4 – 6 mins

(Per Serving)

Calories: 199

Protein: 24 grams

Carbohydrates: 8 grams

Fat: 8 grams

1 teaspoon peanuts, crushed

4 egg whites

1 whole egg

1/4 cup baby spinach

2 tablespoons teriyaki sauce

1/4 teaspoon salt

1/8 teaspoon ground black pepper

> Coat a medium-sized non-stick skillet in cooking spray and place over medium heat. Once the oil is hot, add the peanuts and cook until toasted.

> Meanwhile, in a small mixing bowl, add the eggs, spinach, teriyaki sauce, salt, and pepper. Beat until well combined.

> Pour egg mixture into skillet and scramble. Cook for 4 – 6 minutes, continuing to scramble, until desired consistency.

VEGGIE OMELETTE

Servings: 1

Prep Time: Under 5 mins

Cooking Time: 10 mins

(Per Serving)

Calories: 244

Protein: 27 grams

Carbohydrates: 10 grams

Fat: 10 grams

1/4 cup onion, chopped

1/4 cup green bell pepper, chopped

1/4 cup mushrooms, chopped

5 egg whites

1 whole egg

1 tablespoon skimmed milk

1/4 teaspoon salt

1/8 teaspoon ground black pepper

2 tablespoons Swiss cheese, shredded

> Coat a medium-sized non-stick skillet in cooking spray and place over medium heat. Add the onions, bell peppers, and mushrooms and cook for 3 – 4 minutes, or until tender.

> Meanwhile, in a small mixing bowl, add the eggs, milk, salt, and pepper. Beat until well combined.

> Remove the vegetables from the skillet and set aside. Re-coat the skillet in cooking spray and add the egg mixture. Cook for 2 minutes or until the bottom of the eggs begins to set. Using a spatula, gently lift the edges of the egg and tilt the pan so the uncooked egg flows toward the edges.

> Continue to cook for 2 – 3 minutes or until the centre of the omelette begins to look dry. Add the cheese and vegetables to the centre of the omelette. Using a spatula, fold the omelette in half. Cook for another 1 – 2 minutes, or until cheese is melted and egg has reached desired consistency.

SIMPLE EGG "CUPCAKES"

Servings: 6 (4 muffins per serving)

Prep Time: 5 – 10 mins

Cooking Time: 20 – 30 mins

(Per Serving)

Calories: 169

Protein: 26 grams

Carbohydrates: 4 grams

Fat: 6 grams

1 red bell pepper, diced

2 roma tomatoes, diced

1/4 cup fresh basil leaves, chopped

3 scallions/spring onions, chopped

6 whole eggs

4 cups (32 large) egg whites

salsa, to taste

> Preheat the oven to 375°F/190 °C/Gas Mark 5. Coat 2 12-cup muffin pans in cooking spray.
> In a large mixing bowl, add the bell peppers, tomatoes, basil, and scallions/spring onions, and mix well. In a separate bowl, add your eggs and beat until combined.

> Add 1 tablespoon of egg mixture to each muffin slot. Then evenly divide the vegetable mixture into the muffin slots. Finish by filling each slot to the top with the egg mixture.

> Place in oven and bake for 20 – 30 minutes, or until they are firm on top. Wait until cool to remove from pans. Use some salsa for frosting.

BERRY CHEESECAKE MUFFINS

Servings: 6 (2 muffins per serving)

Prep Time: 3 – 4 mins

Cooking Time: 30 – 35 mins

(Per Serving)

Calories: 208

Protein: 31 grams

Carbohydrates: 14 grams

Fat: 3 grams

1 cup fat-free Greek yogurt

2 tablespoons fat-free cottage cheese

1 tablespoon coconut flour

1/4 cup dried berries

2 eggs

6 scoops vanilla whey protein powder (available Tesco and Holland & Barratt)

1 cup fresh blackberries

> Preheat the oven to 340°F/170 °C/Gas mark 4. Coat a 12-cup muffin pan in cooking spray.

> Place all ingredients except the blackberries in a food processor or blender and process until well combined. Transfer to a large mixing bowl, add the blackberries and gently fold in.

> Pour the batter evenly into the muffin pan, only filling each cup to 3/4 full. Place in oven and bake for 35 minutes, or until a toothpick inserted into the middle comes out clean.

ARTICHOKE FRITTATA

Servings: 2

Prep Time: 5 mins

Cooking Time: 5 – 7 mins

(Per Serving)

Calories: 228

Protein: 20 grams

Carbohydrates: 18 grams

Fat: 10 grams

1 red bell pepper, diced

2 cloves garlic, minced

1/4 teaspoon red pepper flakes

2 whole eggs

4 egg whites

1 (14 ounce/400 grams) can artichoke hearts, rinsed and chopped

1/4 cup low-fat Parmesan cheese, grated

1 teaspoon dried oregano

1/4 teaspoon salt

1/8 teaspoon ground black pepper

> Position an oven rack in the upper third of the oven. Preheat the grill.

> Coat a medium-sized ovenproof skillet in cooking spray and place over medium heat. Add the bell pepper and cook for 2 minutes, or until tender. Stir in the garlic and red pepper flakes. Cook for 1 minute, then transfer to a plate.

> In a medium-sized mixing bowl, add the eggs and beat until well combined. Add the artichoke hearts, Parmesan, oregano, salt, pepper, and bell pepper mixture and mix.

> Recoat the skillet in cooking spray and place back over medium heat. Pour in the egg mixture; tilt the pan around until evenly distributed. Cook for 30 seconds, until bottom starts to set.

> Reduce heat to medium-low and cook until bottom is golden, frequently lifting the edges to let the uncooked egg flow underneath, about 3 – 4 minutes.

> Place the pan under the grill. Cook until top is set, about 2 – 3 minutes. Remove and cut in half.

RED PEPPER & GOAT CHEESE FRITTATA

Servings: 2

Prep Time: Under 5 mins

Cooking Time: 5 – 6 mins

(Per Serving)

Calories: 203

Protein: 20 grams

Carbohydrates: 7 grams

Fat: 11 grams

4 egg whites

2 whole eggs

1 tablespoon fresh oregano, chopped

1/8 teaspoon salt

1/8 teaspoon ground black pepper

1 red bell pepper, sliced

3 scallions/spring onions, thinly sliced (green only)

1/4 cup goat cheese, crumbled

> Position an oven rack in the upper third of the oven. Preheat the grill.
> In a medium-sized mixing bowl, add the eggs, oregano, salt, and pepper and beat until well combined.

> Coat a medium-sized ovenproof skillet in cooking spray and place over medium heat. Add the bell pepper and scallions/spring onions and sauté for 1 minute, until the scallions/spring onions are tender.

> Stir in the egg mixture; tilt the pan around until evenly distributed. Cook for 2 – 3 minutes, frequently lifting the edges to let the uncooked egg flow underneath, until bottom is golden brown. Sprinkle the cheese over top.

> Place the pan under the grill. Cook until top is set, about 2 – 3 minutes. Remove and cut in half.

BREAKFAST RECIPES FOR VEGANS

SPINACH & TOFU SCRAMBLE

Servings: 2

Prep Time: Under 5 mins

Cooking Time: 10 mins

(Per Serving)

Calories: 250

Protein: 27 grams

Carbohydrates: 10 grams

Fat: 13 grams

2 tomatoes, diced

2 cloves garlic, minced

3/4 cup fresh mushrooms, sliced

1 cup spinach, rinsed

2 1/2 cups firm or extra firm tofu, crumbled

1/2 teaspoon low-sodium soy sauce

1 teaspoon lemon juice

salt and ground black pepper, to taste

> Coat a medium-sized skillet in cooking spray and place over medium heat.
> Add the tomatoes, garlic, and mushrooms and sauté for 2 – 3 minutes.

> Reduce heat to medium-low and add the spinach, tofu, soy sauce, and lemon juice. Cover with a tight fitting lid and cook for 5 – 7 minutes, stirring occasionally. Sprinkle with salt and pepper.

TEMPEH HASH

Servings: 4

Prep Time: 5 mins

Cooking Time: 25 mins

(Per Serving)

Calories: 288

Protein: 21 grams

Carbohydrates: 41 grams

Fat: 6 grams

12 ounces/340 grams tempeh, cut into 1/2 inch – 1 1/2 cm cubes

(Tempeh is available in wholefood stores, Holland & Barratt and online)

4 medium potatoes, peeled and diced

1 onion, diced

2 tablespoons low-sodium soy sauce

1/2 teaspoon garlic powder

salt and ground black pepper, to taste

> Place the potatoes in a large pot; add water until the potatoes are just covered. Bring to a boil over medium-high heat and cook for 10 – 15 minutes, or until tender.

> Coat a large skillet in cooking spray and place over medium heat. Add the onions, potatoes, tempeh, and soy sauce and sauté. Stir frequently, ensuring you cook all sides of the tempeh cubes. Remove from heat and add the garlic powder, salt, and pepper.

PB&J OATMEAL

Servings: 4

Prep Time: Under 3 mins

Cooking Time: 5 – 10 mins

(Per Serving)

Calories: 376

Protein: 32 grams

Carbohydrates: 38 grams

Fat: 11 grams

1/3 cup old-fashioned oats

2/3 cup water

1 scoop protein powder (of your choice)

1/2 teaspoon vanilla extract

1 tablespoon peanut butter

1 tablespoon jam

> Add the oats and water to a small saucepan and bring to a boil over medium-high heat.
> Reduce heat to medium-low and let simmer until 90% of the water is absorbed.
> Remove from the heat; add the protein powder and vanilla extract. Whisk together until well combined. Pour oatmeal into a bowl and top with peanut butter and jam.

QUINOA POWER MUFFINS

Servings: 12 (1 muffin per serving)

Prep Time: 10 mins

Cooking Time: 20 – 22 mins

(Per Serving)

Calories: 319

Protein: 10 grams

Carbohydrates: 45 grams

Fat: 17 grams

1 1/2 cups all purpose flour

2 teaspoons baking powder

1/2 teaspoon baking soda

2 packets stevia or other natural sweetener

2 teaspoons cinnamon

1/2 teaspoon salt

3/4 cup wheat bran

1/4 cup oat bran (available in Holland & Barratt)

3 tablespoons ground flax seed

1 1/3 cups almond milk

1/3 cup canola/vegetable oil

1 teaspoon vanilla extract

1 cup quinoa, cooked

1/2 cup walnuts, chopped

1/2 cup vegan chocolate chips (available from online health stores)

1/2 cup hemp seeds (available from Holland & Barratt)

> Preheat oven to 400°F/200 °C/Gas mark 6. Coat a 12-cup muffin pan in cooking spray.

> In a large mixing bowl, add the flour, baking powder, baking soda, stevia, cinnamon, and salt. Whisk together, then pour in the wheat bran, oat bran, and flax seed and whisk until thoroughly combined.

> In a separate bowl, add the almond milk, canola/vegetable oil, and vanilla extract. Whisk together, then pour in the quinoa and whisk to combine. Pour the dry ingredients in and mix together with a wooden or plastic spoon. Fold in the walnuts, chocolate chips, and hemp seeds. Be careful not to over mix, there should still be some chunks.

> Pour the batter into the muffin pan, only filling each cup to 3/4 full. Place in oven and bake for 20 – 22 minutes, or until a toothpick inserted into the middle comes out clean.

MOCHA OATMEAL

Servings: 1

Cooking Time: 5 mins

(Per Serving)

Calories: 170

Protein: 6 grams

Carbohydrates: 30 grams

Fat: 3 gram

1/2 cup old-fashioned oats

1/2 cup water

1/4 cup brewed coffee

1 tablespoon unsweetened cocoa powder

1 teaspoon stevia or other natural sweetener

> Cook oats according to package directions.
> Mix in coffee, cocoa powder and stevia.

PEANUT BUTTER & PROTEIN PANCAKES

Servings: 1

Prep Time: 5 mins

Cooking Time: 5 mins

(Per Serving)

Calories: 397

Protein: 33 grams

Carbohydrates: 51 grams

Fat: 7 grams

1/2 banana, mashed

2 teaspoons peanut butter

1 serving protein powder of your choice (available in Tesco and Holland & Barratt)

1/3 cup whole grain pancake batter

1 teaspoon honey

> In a large mixing bowl, add the banana, peanut butter, protein powder, and batter and mix well.
> Coat a large non-stick skillet in cooking spray and place over medium heat. Divide the batter evenly in half and spoon onto the skillet. Cook, turning when tops are covered with bubbles and edges look cooked. Drizzle honey on top.

TEX-MEX TOFU BREAKFAST TACOS

Servings: 4 (2 tacos per serving)

Prep Time: 5 – 10 mins

Cooking Time: 15 mins

(Per Serving)

Calories: 286

Protein: 16 grams

Carbohydrates: 26 grams

Fat: 9 grams

2 (14 ounce/400 grams) packages soft tofu, drained

3 (6 inch/15 cm) corn tortillas, cut into strips

1/8 teaspoon turmeric

1 jalapeño, seeded and diced

1/2 teaspoon smoked paprika

4 scallions/spring onions trimmed and chopped

1/2 teaspoon salt

1/4 cup fresh coriander, chopped

2 plum tomatoes, diced

1/4 cup vegan cheese, shredded

8 (6 inch/15 cm) corn tortillas, warmed

1/2 cup salsa (optional)

> Coat a large non-stick skillet in cooking spray and place over medium heat. Add the tortilla strips and sauté until golden and crispy, around 6 minutes. Transfer to a plate and set aside.

> Recoat the pan in cooking spray. Add the tofu to the pan and crumble into various sized pieces similar to scrambled eggs. Add the turmeric, jalapeño, paprika, scallions/spring onions, and salt and stir until well combined.

> Cook until the remaining water in the tofu has cooked off and it has a tender consistency, about 4 – 6 minutes. Add the coriander, tomatoes, cheese, and tortilla strips. Stir until well combined. Continue stirring until cheese has melted, around 2 minutes.

> Divide into 4 equal portions, then divide each portion between 2 corn tortillas. Top each taco with 1 tablespoon salsa.

ENTRÉE RECIPES FOR VEGETARIANS

MEXICAN ENCHILADA CASSEROLE

Servings: 8

Prep Time: 5 mins

Cooking Time: 15 – 20 mins

(Per Serving)

Calories: 293

Protein: 19 grams

Carbohydrates: 47 grams

Fat: 4 grams

2 cups onion, chopped

1 1/2 cups red bell pepper, chopped

2 cloves garlic, minced

3/4 cup salsa

2 teaspoons ground cumin

2 (15 ounce/425 grams) cans black beans, drained

12 (6 inch/15 cm) whole grain tortillas

2 cups low-fat cheddar cheese, shredded

3 tomatoes, chopped

1/2 cup fat-free sour cream

> Preheat the oven to 350°F/180 °C/Gas mark 4.

> Coat a large skillet in cooking spray and place over medium heat. Add the onion, pepper, garlic, salsa, cumin, and black beans and bring to a simmer. Stir frequently and allow to cook for 3 minutes.

> In a 9 x 13 inch/23 x 33 cm baking dish, arrange 6 of the tortillas along the bottom, overlapping as necessary. Spread out half of the mixture and sprinkle half of the cheese on top. Repeat with the remaining tortillas, bean mixture and cheese.

> Cover dish with foil and place in the oven to bake for 15 minutes. Remove from oven, serve with tomatoes and sour cream.

THREE-CHEESE LASAGNE

Servings: 10

Prep Time: 5 mins

Cooking Time: 1 hr 20 mins

(Per Serving)

Calories: 343

Protein: 31 grams

Carbohydrates: 25 grams

Fat: 15 grams

1 (8 ounce/225 grams) package whole grain lasagne noodles, cooked

3 eggs

3 cups low-fat cottage cheese

1/2 cup low-fat Parmesan cheese, grated

1 cup fresh spinach

3 cups pasta sauce

3 cups low-fat mozzarella cheese, grated

> Preheat oven to 325°F/160 °C/Gas mark 3. Coat a 9 x 13 inch/23 x 33 cm baking dish in cooking spray.
> In a large mixing bowl, add the eggs and beat. Add the cottage cheese and Parmesan cheese and mix.

> Place 1 layer of the noodles along the bottom of the baking dish. Top with half of the spinach, press down slightly. Top with another layer of noodles. Top with the cottage cheese mixture, then top with the remaining spinach. Add the last of the noodles and top with the pasta sauce and mozzarella.

> Spray some foil with cooking spray to prevent from sticking and cover the baking dish. Secure tightly around the sides, being careful not to press down on the centre.

> Place in oven and bake for 1 hour and 10 minutes. Remove foil and bake 3 – 5 more minutes or until top is lightly browned. Remove from oven and let sit for 10 – 15 minutes before serving.

TABBOULEH SALAD

Servings: 4

Prep Time: 5 – 10 mins

Cooking Time: 30 mins

(Per Serving)

Calories: 539

Protein: 27 grams

Carbohydrates: 71 grams

Fat: 13 grams

1 1/4 cups bulgur wheat

1/4 cup prepared pesto

3 tablespoons lemon juice

2 cups cherry tomatoes, chopped

3/4 cup feta cheese, crumbled

1 (15 ounce/425 grams) can chickpeas, drained and rinsed

1/3 cup scallions/spring onions, chopped

2 tablespoons fresh parsley, minced

1/4 teaspoon ground black pepper

2 cups edamame beans

> Bring 2 cups of water to a boil. In a large pot or bowl, add the bulgur wheat and the boiling water, cover and set aside for 30 minutes. Drain.

> Meanwhile, in a small mixing bowl, add the pesto and lemon juice and whisk until combined.

> Pour the pesto mixture over the bulgur. Add the tomatoes, feta, chickpeas, scallions/spring onions, parsley, pepper, and edamame. Toss to combine.

HIGH PROTEIN MAC & CHEESE

Servings: 4

Prep Time: 5 mins

Cooking Time: 40 mins

(Per Serving)

Calories: 359

Protein: 22 grams

Carbohydrates: 61 grams

Fat: 4 grams

1 cup (dry) whole grain elbow macaroni noodles, cooked (Tesco)

1 tablespoon margarine

1/4 cup whole grain flour

2 1/2 cups skimmed milk

2 ounces/55 grams light pasteurized processed cheese, cubed

1/2 cup low-fat cheddar cheese, shredded

1 teaspoon Dijon mustard

salt and ground black pepper, to taste

2 tablespoons plain bread crumbs

> Preheat oven to 350°F/180 °C/Gas mark 4.

> Place a medium-sized saucepan over medium-low heat. Add the margarine and melt, once melted add the flour and cook for 1 minute, stirring constantly.

> Stir in the milk and heat to boiling. Stir constantly, until thickened, about 1 minute. Add the processed cheese, cheddar, and mustard, continue to stir until cheese is melted.

> Place macaroni in a 2-quart/2.5 litre casserole dish. Pour the sauce over and mix. Season with salt and pepper, then sprinkle bread crumbs over.

> Place in oven and bake for 30 – 40 minutes, or until cheese is bubbly and crust is golden brown.

APPLE CHEDDAR PANINI

Servings: 4

Prep Time: Under 5 mins

Cooking Time: 15 mins

(Per Serving)

Calories: 344

Protein: 23 grams

Carbohydrates: 48 grams

Fat: 7 grams

8 slices whole grain bread

4 tablespoons low-fat honey mustard

2 apples, thinly sliced

8 ounces/225 grams low-fat cheddar cheese, thinly sliced

> If you have a panini press or countertop grill, preheat on medium heat. If not, coat a skillet in cooking spray and place over medium heat.

> Spread 1 tablespoon of the honey mustard evenly over each slice of bread, and then evenly divide the apple slices and cheese to make 4 sandwiches.

> Place on the skillet and top with a lid or something to press down on sandwich. Cook for 2 – 3 minutes and flip, apply a fresh coat of cooking spray when flipping.

GREEK PASTA SALAD

Servings: 6

Prep Time: 5 mins

Cooking Time: 20 mins

(Per Serving)

Calories: 501

Protein: 19 grams

Carbohydrates: 73 grams

Fat: 13 grams

8 ounces/225 grams whole grain bow-tie pasta/farfalle

2 medium tomatoes, chopped

2 cloves garlic, minced

1 tablespoon extra-virgin olive oil

2 tablespoons red wine vinegar

1 (15 ounce/425 grams) can chickpeas, drained and rinsed

1 medium cucumber, chopped into 1/2-inch – 1 ½ cm pieces

1/2 cup low-fat feta cheese, crumbled

1/3 cup pitted Kalamata olives, quartered

2 tablespoons fresh oregano, chopped

> Cook pasta according to package directions.

> Meanwhile, in a large mixing bowl, add the tomatoes, garlic, oil, and vinegar. Mix well.

> Drain the pasta and rinse with cold water until chilled. Pour the pasta over the tomato mixture. Add the chickpeas, cucumber, feta, olives, and oregano. Toss to combine.

BEAN BOLOGNESE

Servings: 4

Prep Time: 5 mins

Cooking Time: 25 mins

(Per Serving)

Calories: 357

Protein: 17 grams

Carbohydrates: 59 grams

Fat: 2 grams

1 small onion, chopped

1/2 cup carrots, chopped

1/4 cup celery, chopped

1/2 teaspoon salt

1 (14 ounce/400 grams) can kidney beans, drained and rinsed

4 cloves garlic, chopped

1 bay leaf

1/2 cup white wine

1 (14 ounces/400 grams) can diced tomatoes, with liquid

1/4 cup fresh parsley, chopped

8 ounces/225 grams whole grain fettuccine

1/4 cup low-fat Parmesan cheese, grated

> Coat a medium saucepan in cooking spray and place over medium heat. Add the onion, carrot, celery, and salt and mix well. Cover and let cook, stirring occasionally, for 10 minutes, or until vegetables have softened.

> Meanwhile, in a small mixing bowl, add 1/2 cup of the beans and mash with a fork.

> Add the garlic and bay leaf to the saucepan. Cook for 15 seconds, until fragrant. Add the wine and increase the heat to high and boil for 3 – 4 minutes, or until wine is mostly evaporated. Add the tomatoes, parsley, and the mashed beans. Reduce heat to medium and simmer, stirring occasionally, for 5 – 6 minutes, or until sauce has thickened.

> Add the remaining beans and cook until heated through, 2 – 3 minutes. Remove from heat and remove the bay leaf.

> Meanwhile, cook the pasta according to package directions. Pour the drained pasta into the sauce and toss to coat. Divide into 4 portions, top each portion with 1 tablespoon Parmesan cheese.

SPEEDY PITTA PIZZA

Servings: 1

Prep Time: 5 mins

Cooking Time: 3 – 5 mins

(Per Serving)

Calories: 293

Protein: 32 grams

Carbohydrates: 28 grams

Fat: 9 grams

1 whole grain pitta

1 cup baby spinach

1/2 (14 ounce/400 grams) package low-fat extra-firm tofu, cubed

1/4 cup low-fat mozzarella cheese, shredded

1/2 lemon, juiced

salt and ground black pepper, to taste

> Top the pitta with the spinach, tofu, and mozzarella. Season with salt and pepper and sprinkle with lemon juice.
> Place in toaster oven (4 – 5 minutes) or microwave (2 – 3 minutes) until cheese has melted to desired consistency.

EGGPLANT/AUBERGINE PARMESAN

Servings: 6

Prep Time: 5 – 10 mins

Cooking Time: 1 hr 15 mins

(Per Serving)

Calories: 255

Protein: 19 grams

Carbohydrates: 30 grams

Fat: 6 grams

2 pounds/900 grams eggplant/aubergine, peeled and sliced thickly

4 egg whites

1 tablespoon water

1/2 cup seasoned bread crumbs

1 cup low-fat Parmesan cheese, shredded

1/2 cup fresh basil leaves, chopped

1/2 teaspoon red pepper flakes

2 teaspoons minced garlic

1/4 teaspoon salt

2 cups fat-free ricotta cheese

3 cups pasta sauce (of your choice)

1/2 cup low-fat mozzarella cheese, shredded

> Preheat the oven to 375°F/190 °C/Gas mark 5. Coat 2 large baking sheets in cooking spray.

> In a small mixing bowl, add 3 of the egg whites and 1 tablespoon water. In a separate small mixing bowl, add the bread crumbs and 1/4 cup of the Parmesan cheese. One at a time, dip the eggplant/aubergine slices in the egg mixture, then in the breadcrumb mixture to coat.

> Place the eggplant slices on the baking sheet and bake for 30 minutes, or until golden, turning the eggplants/aubergines and rotating the baking sheets after 15 minutes.

> Meanwhile, in a medium-sized mixing bowl, add the basil, red pepper flakes, garlic, salt, ricotta cheese, 1/4 cup of the Parmesan, and the remaining egg white. Mix well.

> Coat a deep baking dish in cooking spray. Start by creating a layer of ½ cup pasta sauce on the bottom of the pan, followed by a layer of eggplant/aubergine. Top with about ¾ cup pasta sauce, followed by half of the ricotta mixture, then 1/3rd of the mozzarella. Repeat this layering process once more. Finish by sprinkling mozzarella cheese over top.

> Cover tightly with aluminium foil coated in cooking spray. Bake for 35 minutes. Remove foil and top with the remaining 1/3rd mozzarella. Return to oven for another 10 minutes, or until sauce is bubbly and cheese is melted.

SEVEN LAYER BEAN PIE

Servings: 4

Prep Time: 15 mins

Cooking Time: 40 mins

(Per Serving)

Calories: 401

Protein: 26 grams

Carbohydrates: 62 grams

Fat: 6 grams

2 (15 ounce/425 grams) cans pinto beans, drained and rinsed

1 cup salsa, divided

2 cloves garlic, minced

2 tablespoons fresh coriander, chopped

1 (15 ounce/425 grams) can black beans, drained and rinsed

1/2 cup tomatoes, chopped

7 (8 inch/20 cm) whole grain tortillas

2 cups low-fat cheddar cheese, shredded

6 tablespoons fat-free sour cream

> Preheat the oven to 400°F/200 °C/Gas mark 6. Coat a pie plate or tart dish in cooking spray.

> In a large mixing bowl, add the pinto beans and mash. Add 3/4 cup of the salsa and the garlic and mix until well combined.

> In a separate mixing bowl, add the black beans, coriander, tomatoes, and remaining 1/4 cup salsa. Mix until well combined.

> To construct the pie, place 1 tortilla down on the pie plate, top with 3/4 cup of the pinto bean mixture, make sure to leave 1/2 an inch/ 1 ½ cm of room on the edges. Top with 1/4 cup of the cheese, then another tortilla. For the next layer spread 2/3 cup of the black bean mixture out, then top with 1/4 cup of the cheese. Repeat this layering process twice.

> After topping with the final tortilla, spread out the remaining pinto bean mixture and cheese over top. Cover with foil and place in oven for 40 minutes.

> Remove from oven and cut into 6 wedges. Serve each wedge with 1 tablespoon of sour cream.

ENTRÉE RECIPES FOR VEGANS

TEMPEH TACOS WITH AVOCADO-LIME CREAM SAUCE

Servings: 2 (2 tacos per serving)

Prep Time: 2 hrs

Cooking Time: 2 – 3 mins

(Per Serving)

Calories: 523

Protein: 24 grams

Carbohydrates: 44 grams

Fat: 33 grams

1 (6 ounce/170 grams) block tempeh, cubed (available in wholefood stores or online)

1 teaspoon extra-virgin olive oil

1 teaspoon low-sodium soy sauce

1 teaspoon maple syrup

1/4 teaspoon ground black pepper

1 teaspoon vegan Worcestershire sauce

1/2 teaspoon barbecue seasoning

1/4 teaspoon cumin

1/8 cup cashews, soaked in water overnight

1/2 small avocado

2 tablespoons lime juice

1/4 cup water

1/2 teaspoon seasoned salt

4 (6 inch/15 cm) corn tortillas

4 tablespoons salsa

> In a large ziplock bag, combine the tempeh, olive oil, soy sauce, maple syrup, pepper, Worcestershire sauce, barbecue seasoning, and cumin. Seal and toss, place in refrigerator for at least 2 hours or overnight.

> Heat a large skillet over medium-high heat and coat in cooking spray. Add the tempeh and sauté for a couple minutes, until browned and crispy.

> Meanwhile, drain the cashews. In a blender or food processor, add the cashews, avocado, lime juice, water, and seasoned salt. Blend until smooth.

> Top tortillas with equal portions of the tempeh and desired amount of lime sauce and salsa.

TOFU PUTTANESCA

Servings: 2

Prep Time: 5 mins

Cooking Time: 20 mins

(Per Serving)

Calories: 225

Protein: 21 grams

Carbohydrates: 11 grams

Fat: 12 grams

1 pound/450 grams extra firm tofu, cubed

4 cloves garlic, thinly sliced

1/2 teaspoon crushed red pepper flakes

4 roma tomatoes, diced

2 tablespoons fresh thyme, chopped

2 tablespoons fresh oregano, chopped

1/2 cup mixed olives, chopped

1 tablespoon capers

salt and ground black pepper, to taste

> Coat a large skillet in cooking spray and place over medium heat. Once hot, add the garlic and sauté for 1 – 2 minutes, until lightly browned.

> Add the tofu and red pepper flakes and sauté for about 10 minutes, or until tofu is browned. Add another coat of cooking spray after a couple minutes to prevent burning.

> Add the tomatoes, thyme, and oregano and cook for about 5 minutes, or until tomatoes have broken down. Add the olives, capers, salt, and pepper and sauté for another minute or until flavours have mixed.

BLACK BEAN BURGERS

Servings: 3 (1 burger per serving)

Prep Time: 5 – 10 mins

Cooking Time: 5 – 8 mins

(Per Serving)

Calories: 280

Protein: 15 grams

Carbohydrates: 57 grams

Fat: 2 grams

1 can (15 ounce/425 grams) black beans

1/2 onion, diced

1 teaspoon garlic powder

1 teaspoon onion powder

1/2 teaspoon seasoned salt

1/2 cup whole grain flour

2 slices whole grain bread, crumbled

> Coat a large skillet in cooking spray and place over medium heat. Add the onions and sauté until soft, about 3 – 5 minutes.

> Meanwhile, in a large mixing bowl, add the black beans and mash until only a few chunks remain. Add the onions, garlic powder, onion powder, salt, and whole grain bread. Add the flour in slowly, a couple of tablespoons at a time, to prevent clumping.

> Divide into 3 portions and form into patties. Re-coat the skillet you used for onions in cooking spray and fry the patties until slightly firm, 2 – 3 minutes on each side.

QUICK BEAN & SQUASH STEW

Servings: 4

Prep Time: 10 mins

Cooking Time: 20 – 25 mins

(Per Serving)

Calories: 303

Protein: 15 grams

Carbohydrates: 62 grams

Fat: 1 gram

1 1/2 cups onion, chopped

1 1/2 cups green bell pepper, chopped

2 teaspoons minced garlic

1 tablespoon whole grain flour

2 cups butternut squash, peeled and cubed

2 (16 ounce/450 grams) cans low-sodium diced tomatoes, with liquid

1 (15 ounce/425 grams) can red kidney beans, drained and rinsed

1 (13 ounce/400 grams) can baby lima beans, drained and rinsed

salt and ground black pepper, to taste

> Coat a large saucepan in cooking spray and place over medium heat.
> Add the onion, bell pepper, and garlic and sauté until tender, about 7 minutes. Stir in the flour and cook for 1 minute.
> Add the remaining ingredients and bring to a boil. Reduce heat and simmer 10 – 15 minutes, or until beans are tender.

RAW ALMOND FLAXSEED BURGERS

Servings: 2 (2 burgers per serving)

Prep Time: 5 – 8 mins

(Per Serving)

Calories: 280

Protein: 9 grams

Carbohydrates: 11 grams

Fat: 24 grams

1 clove garlic

1 cup raw almonds

1/2 cup ground flaxseed (available in Holland & Barratt)

2 tablespoons balsamic vinegar

1 tablespoon coconut oil

1/4 teaspoon salt

> Place all ingredients in a food processor or blender and blend until well combined.

> Remove from food processor. Divide mixture evenly and shape into four patties.

SQUASH & TOFU CURRY

Servings: 4

Prep Time: 5 – 10 mins

Cooking Time: 25 mins

(Per Serving)

Calories: 269

Protein: 16 grams

Carbohydrates: 33 grams

Fat: 10 grams

2 tablespoons curry powder

1/2 teaspoon salt

1/4 teaspoon ground black pepper

1 pound/450 grams low-fat extra-firm tofu, cubed

1 large marrow, halved, seeded and cut into 1-inch/2 ½ cm cubes

1 medium onion, chopped

2 teaspoons fresh ginger, grated

1 (14 ounce/400 grams) can light coconut milk

1 teaspoon brown sugar

8 cups kale, chopped and stems removed

1 tablespoon lime juice

> In a small mixing bowl, add the curry powder, salt, and pepper. Combine to make seasoning. In a large mixing bowl, add the tofu and 1 teaspoon of the seasoning, toss to coat.

> Coat a large non-stick skillet in cooking spray and place over medium-high heat. Add the tofu and cook, rotating every 2 minutes, until browned, about 8 minutes total. Transfer to a plate and set aside.

> Recoat the skillet in cooking spray, add the marrow, onion, ginger and the rest of the seasoning. Cook, stirring occasionally, until the vegetables are tender and lightly browned, about 5 minutes.

> Stir in the coconut milk and brown sugar, bring to a boil. Add half of the kale and cook until slightly wilted, about 1 minute. Add the remaining kale and cook for an additional minute.

> Place the tofu back in the pan and mix well. Cover and cook, stirring occasionally, until the squash is tender, about 4 – 5 minutes. Remove from heat and stir in lime juice.

TOFU CHILLI

Servings: 4

Prep Time: 10 – 15 mins

Cooking Time: 45 mins

(Per Serving)

Calories: 334

Protein: 23 grams

Carbohydrates: 50 grams

Fat: 6 grams

1 (14 ounce/400 grams) package extra-firm tofu, drained and crumbled

1 medium onion, diced

1 green bell pepper, diced

3 cloves garlic, minced

1 cup mushrooms, sliced

3 tablespoons chilli powder

1/4 teaspoon salt

1/4 teaspoon ground black pepper

1/4 teaspoon cayenne pepper

1/2 teaspoon cumin

1 (14 ounce/400 grams) can tomato sauce/passata or puree

1 (28 ounce/800 grams) can diced tomatoes, with liquid

1 (28 ounce/800 grams) can kidney beans, drained and rinsed

1 teaspoon stevia or other natural sweetener

> Coat a large pot in cooking spray and place over medium heat. Add the tofu and sauté for about 3 minutes, until lightly browned.

> Add the onions, green peppers, garlic, mushrooms, chilli powder, salt, pepper, cayenne, and cumin. Cook for about 5 minutes, or until veggies are just tender.

> Stir in the tomato sauce/passata, diced tomatoes, kidney beans, and stevia. Cover and reduce heat to medium-low. Let simmer for at least 45 minutes, until chilli reaches desired consistency and flavour.

WALNUT PENNE PASTA

Servings: 4

Prep Time: 5 mins

Cooking Time: 15 – 20 mins

(Per Serving)

Calories: 349

Protein: 20 grams

Carbohydrates: 49 grams

Fat: 11 grams

8/225 grams ounces (dry) whole grain penne

2 cloves garlic, minced

1/3 cup walnuts, chopped

3 /4 cup sun-dried tomatoes in oil, drained and chopped

1 tablespoon fresh basil, chopped

1 pound low-fat extra-firm tofu, drained and crumbled

1/8 teaspoon salt

> Cook pasta according to package directions.
> Meanwhile, in a large mixing bowl, add the garlic, walnuts, sun-dried tomatoes, basil, tofu, and salt. Mix well. Add the cooked pasta, toss until well combined. Can be served warm or chilled.

CHIPOTLE BROCCOLI & TOFU STIR-FRY

Servings: 4

Prep Time: Under 5 mins

Cooking Time: 15 – 20 mins

(Per Serving)

Calories: 173

Protein: 19 grams

Carbohydrates: 15 grams

Fat: 4 grams

2 (14 ounce/400 grams) packages low-fat extra-firm tofu, drained and cubed

1/2 teaspoon salt, divided

6 cups broccoli florets

1 cup orange juice

1 tablespoon chipotle chillies in adobo, minced (available in Asda, Tesco)

1/2 cup fresh coriander, chopped

> Coat a large non-stick skillet in cooking spray and place over medium-high heat. Add the tofu and 1/4 teaspoon of the salt. Stir occasionally and cook for 7 – 9 minutes, or until golden brown on all sides. Transfer to a plate and set aside.

> Recoat the skillet in cooking spray, add the broccoli and the remaining 1/4 teaspoon salt. Sauté for 1 – 2 minutes, until the broccoli is bright green. Add the orange juice and chipotle chillies. Continue to sauté for 2 – 3 more minutes, until broccoli is just tender.

> Return the tofu to the pan and cook for about 1 – 2 minutes, until tofu is heated through. Remove from heat and stir in the coriander.

SPICY SZECHUAN TOFU STIR-FRY

Servings: 4

Prep Time: 10 mins

Cooking Time: 15 – 20 mins

(Per Serving)

Calories: 180

Protein: 20 grams

Carbohydrates: 22 grams

Fat: 4 grams

2 (14 ounce/400 grams) packages low-fat extra-firm tofu, drained and cubed

1/4 cup low-sodium soy sauce

1 tablespoon tomato paste

2 teaspoons balsamic vinegar

1/2 teaspoon stevia or other natural sweetener

1/4 teaspoon red pepper flakes

2 tablespoons plus 1 teaspoon cornstarch/cornflour, divided

1/2 cup water, divided

4 cups green beans, cut into halves

4 cloves garlic, minced

2 teaspoons fresh ginger, minced

> In a small mixing bowl, add the soy sauce, tomato paste, vinegar, stevia, red pepper flakes, 1 teaspoon cornstarch/cornflour, and 1/4 cup of the water. Whisk together until well combined and set aside. In a separate bowl, add the tofu and 2 tablespoons cornstarch/cornflour, toss to coat.

> Coat a large skillet in cooking spray and place over medium-high heat. Add the tofu and cook, stirring occasionally, for about 4 – 5 minutes, until lightly browned and crispy on all sides. Transfer to a plate and set aside.

> Recoat the skillet in cooking spray and reduce heat to medium. Add the green beans, garlic, and ginger and sauté for 1 minute. Add the remaining 1/4 cup water, cover and let cook for 3 – 4 minutes, or until green beans are tender.

> Give the soy sauce mixture a quick whisk and pour over the green beans. Cook, stirring constantly, for 1 – 2 minutes, or until sauce has thickened. Stir in the tofu and cook until heated through, about 1 – 2 minutes.

SIDES

THE FOLLOWING SIDE DISHES can be included with your meals, not only to add some excitement and variety of taste, but also to help you meet your nutritional requirements. Be creative, mix and match sides with main dishes, and you'll discover food combinations that you'll come back to time and time again.

SIDE RECIPES FOR VEGETARIANS

SHERRY-ASIAGO CREAM BRUSSELS SPROUTS

Servings: 4

Prep Time: 5 mins

Cooking Time: 15 – 20 mins

(Per Serving)

Calories: 112

Protein: 8 grams

Carbohydrates: 15 grams

Fat: 12 grams

1 pound/450 grams Brussels sprouts, trimmed and halved

2 tablespoons shallots, minced

1 tablespoon all-purpose flour

2/3 cup skim milk

2 tablespoons dry sherry

1/3 cup Asiago cheese, shredded (available in Tescos)

1/4 teaspoon salt

1/8 teaspoon ground black pepper

> Place a large saucepan with about 1 inch/2 ½ cm of water over medium-high heat and bring to a boil. Place the Brussels sprouts in a steamer basket and steam until tender, about 7 – 9 minutes.

> Meanwhile, coat a small saucepan in cooking spray and place over medium heat. Add the shallots and sauté until tender, 1 – 2 minutes. Add the flour and stir to combine.

> Pour in the milk and sherry and bring to a simmer, whisking constantly. Reduce heat to medium-low and simmer, whisking often, until thickened for about 3 minutes.

> Remove from heat, stir in the cheese, salt, and pepper. Place the Brussels sprouts in a large bowl and pour in sauce, toss to coat.

SAUTÉED SPINACH

Servings: 2

Prep Time: Under 5 mins

Cooking Time: 2 – 3 mins

(Per Serving)

Calories: 69

Protein: 4 grams

Carbohydrates: 14 grams

Fat: 1 gram

6 cups (10 ounce/280 grams bag) fresh spinach, rinsed

2 tablespoons golden raisins

1 tablespoon pine nuts

2 cloves garlic, minced

2 teaspoons balsamic vinegar

1/8 teaspoon salt

ground black pepper, to taste

1 tablespoon low-fat Parmesan cheese, shredded

> Coat a large non-stick skillet or saucepan in cooking spray and place over medium-high heat. Once hot, add the raisins, pine nuts, and garlic. Sauté until fragrant, about 30 seconds.

> Stir in the spinach and sauté until just wilted, about 2 minutes. Remove from heat; add the vinegar, salt, and pepper. Toss and sprinkle with Parmesan.

SIDE RECIPES FOR VEGANS

SALTY EDAMAME

Servings: 4

Cooking Time: 5 – 8 mins

(Per Serving)

Calories: 50

Protein: 4 grams

Carbohydrates: 5 grams

Fat: 1 gram

1 cup edamame, in the shell

salt, to taste

> Place a large saucepan over medium-low heat. Add 2 quarts water and edamame. Cover and let simmer until tender, about 5 – 8 minutes.
> Drain and sprinkle with salt.

THREE BEAN SALAD

Servings: 2 – 3

Prep Time: 5 mins (4 hrs in the fridge)

(Per Serving)

Calories: 195

Protein: 6 grams

Carbohydrates: 22 grams

Fat: 9 grams

1 (16 ounce/450 grams) can green beans, drained and rinsed

1 (16 ounce/450 grams) can cannellini or borlotti beans, drained and rinsed

1 (16 ounce/450 grams) can red kidney beans, drained and rinsed

4 tablespoons stevia or other natural sweetener

2/3 cup vinegar

1/4 cup vegetable oil

1/2 teaspoon salt

1/2 teaspoon ground black pepper

1 onion, sliced thinly

> In a large mixing bowl, add the stevia, vinegar, oil, salt, and pepper and whisk together to make the dressing. Pour in the beans and onions and toss to coat.

> Cover and place in refrigerator for at least 4 hours or overnight to chill, best if stirred occasionally. If desired, you can drain the excess liquid before serving.

EASY WHITE BEAN SALAD

Servings: 6

Prep Time: 5 mins

Cooling Time: 30 mins

(Per Serving)

Calories: 143

Protein: 6 grams

Carbohydrates: 25 grams

Fat: 11 grams

2 (15 ounce/425 grams) cans lima beans, drained and rinsed

1/2 pound/225 grams plum tomatoes, chopped

1/2 cup fresh basil leaves, chopped

1 teaspoon salt

1/2 teaspoon ground black pepper

3 cloves garlic, minced

4 tablespoons extra-virgin olive oil

> Coat a large non-stick skillet in cooking spray and place over medium heat. Add the garlic and sauté until just lightly browned, 1 – 2 minutes.
> Meanwhile, in a large salad bowl, add the beans, tomatoes, basil, salt, and pepper. Pour the garlic and oil over the salad and toss to combine.

> Let the salad sit at least 30 minutes to allow flavours to combine.

ITALIAN STYLE SNAP PEAS

Servings: 4

Prep Time: Under 5 mins

Cooking Time: 25 mins

(Per Serving)

Calories: 91

Protein: 4 grams

Carbohydrates: 14 grams

Fat: 3 grams

1 large leek (white part only), washed, halved lengthwise and cut into 2 inch/5 cm strips

1 pound/450 grams sugar snap peas, trimmed

2 teaspoons extra-virgin olive oil

1/2 teaspoon salt

1 cup cherry tomatoes, halved

1 teaspoon dried oregano

> Preheat oven to 425°F/220 °C/Gas mark 7. Coat a baking sheet in cooking spray.
> In a large mixing bowl, add the leeks, peas, olive oil, and salt. Toss to combine.

> Spread mixture out on baking sheet and roast for 15 minutes. Stir in the tomatoes and roast for 10 more minutes, or until vegetables start to brown. Sprinkle with oregano.

CORN & EDAMAME SUCCOTASH

Servings: 4

Prep Time: 5 mins

Cooking Time: 10 mins

(Per Serving)

Calories: 126

Protein: 6 grams

Carbohydrates: 15 grams

Fat: 5 grams

1 tablespoon canola/vegetable oil

1/2 cup red bell pepper, chopped

1/4 cup onion, chopped

2 cloves garlic, minced

2 cups fresh corn kernels

3 tablespoons dry white wine

1 1/2 cups edamame beans, cooked according to package

2 tablespoons rice vinegar

2 tablespoons fresh parsley, chopped

2 tablespoons fresh basil, chopped

1/2 teaspoon salt

1/4 teaspoon ground black pepper

> Place a large non-stick skillet over medium heat, add the oil and heat. Once hot, add the bell pepper, onion, and garlic. Sauté until vegetables are tender, about 2 minutes.

> Stir in the corn, white wine, and edamame and continue to sauté for about 4 minutes, until flavours are well combined.

> Remove from heat and stir in the vinegar, parsley, basil, salt, and pepper.

ASIAN GINGER BROCCOLI

Servings: 4

Prep Time: Under 5 mins

Cooking Time: 6 mins

(Per Serving)

Calories: 73

Protein: 4 grams

Carbohydrates: 8 grams

Fat: 4 grams

1 tablespoon canola/vegetable oil

2 tablespoons minced garlic

4 teaspoons fresh ginger, minced

5 cups broccoli crowns, halved

3 tablespoons water

1 tablespoon rice vinegar

> Heat the oil in a large skillet over medium-high heat. Add the garlic and ginger and sauté until fragrant, about 45 seconds. Add the broccoli and sauté until broccoli is bright green, about 2 minutes.

> Pour in the water, stir and cover. Reduce heat to medium and cook until broccoli is tender, about 3 minutes. Toss with vinegar.

SAUTÉED CAULIFLOWER

Servings: 4

Prep Time: Under 5 mins

Cooking Time: 10 mins

(Per Serving)

Calories: 38

Protein: 3 grams

Carbohydrates: 8 grams

Fat: 0 grams

4 cups cauliflower florets, chopped

2 tablespoons water

2 teaspoons red wine vinegar

1 cup cherry tomatoes, halved

2 tablespoons fresh parsley, chopped

1 tablespoon minced garlic

1/4 teaspoon salt

1/4 teaspoon ground black pepper

> Coat a large non-stick skillet in cooking spray and place over medium heat. Add the cauliflower, cover and cook for 4 minutes, stirring occasionally.

> Pour in the water and vinegar, stir to combine and cover. Let cook until cauliflower is golden and tender and the liquid has evaporated, about 4 more minutes.

> Add the tomatoes, parsley, garlic, salt, and pepper. Cook until tomatoes have softened and flavours have combined, about 2 more minutes.

GARLIC ROSEMARY MUSHROOMS

Servings: 4

Prep Time: Under mins

Cooking Time: 10 mins

(Per Serving)

Calories: 52

Protein: 6 grams

Carbohydrates: 7 grams

Fat: 1 gram

1 pound/450 grams mixed mushrooms, cut into 1/4-inch/1 cm slices

2 cloves garlic, finely chopped

1/2 tablespoon fresh rosemary, chopped

1/4 teaspoon salt

1/8 teaspoon ground black pepper

1/4 cup dry white wine

> Coat a large skillet in cooking spray and place over medium heat. Add the mushrooms, garlic, rosemary, salt, and pepper.
> Cook until mushrooms are soft, about 8 minutes, stir occasionally. Pour in the wine and stir, cook until mostly evaporated, 1 – 2 minutes.

MEDITERRANEAN BROCCOLI

Servings: 4

Prep Time: 5 mins

Cooking Time: 10 – 12 mins

(Per Serving)

Calories: 8

Protein: 2 grams

Carbohydrates: 8 grams

Fat: 4 grams

4 cups broccoli florets

1 cup cherry tomatoes

1 tablespoon extra-virgin olive oil

2 cloves garlic, minced

1/4 teaspoon salt

1/2 teaspoon lemon zest

1 tablespoon lemon juice

1/4 cup black olives, pitted and sliced

1 teaspoon dried oregano

2 teaspoons capers, rinsed

> Preheat oven to 450°F/230 °C/Gas mark 8. Coat a baking sheet in cooking spray.

> In a large mixing bowl, add the broccoli, tomatoes, olive oil, garlic, and salt and toss to coat. Spread out on the baking sheet and bake until broccoli begins to brown, 10 – 12 minutes.

> Meanwhile, take the large mixing bowl and add the lemon zest, lemon juice, olives, oregano, and capers. Add the cooked vegetables and stir to combine.

ASPARAGUS STIR-FRY

Servings: 4

Prep Time: Under 5 mins

Cooking Time: 8 – 10 mins

(Per Serving)

Calories: 30

Protein: 3 grams

Carbohydrates: 6 grams

Fat: 0 grams

1/4 medium onion, chopped

1 pound fresh asparagus, trimmed

1 clove garlic, thinly sliced

2 teaspoons teriyaki sauce

> Coat a large skillet in cooking spray and place over medium heat. Add the onions and sauté until tender, 1 – 2 minutes.

> Add the asparagus and garlic and sauté for 3 – 5 minutes, until asparagus is slightly tender. Pour in the teriyaki sauce and stir for an additional minute to let the flavours combine.

EGGPLANT/AUBERGINE "BACON"

Servings: 4

Prep Time: 1 hr. including marination

Cooking Time: 45 mins

(Per Serving)

Calories: 127

Protein: 2 grams

Carbohydrates: 16 grams

Fat: 7 grams

1 large eggplant/aubergine, sliced lengthwise into 1/4-inch/1 cm thick (or less) slices

2 tablespoons tamari (available in Tescos)

2 tablespoons maple syrup

2 tablespoons apple cider vinegar

2 tablespoons extra-virgin olive oil

1 teaspoon chilli powder

1/4 teaspoon smoked paprika

1/8 teaspoon ground black pepper

> Place all of the ingredients in a large ziplock bag, seal and shake to coat. Place in refrigerator and marinate for at least an hour.

> Preheat oven to 350°F/180 °C/Gas mark 4.

> Lay slices out on a baking sheet and bake, occasionally basting with the marinade, for about 45 minutes or until desired level of crispiness.

CARROT FRIES

Servings: 1

Prep Time: Under 5 mins

Cooking Time: 40 – 45 mins

(Per Serving)

Calories: 101

Protein: 1 gram

Carbohydrates: 7 grams

Fat: 5 grams

2 large carrots, cut into fry shape wedges

1 teaspoon coconut oil (available in Tesco and Holland & Barratt)

1/4 teaspoon salt

1/8 teaspoon ground black pepper

> Preheat oven to 450°F/230 °C/Gas mark 8. Coat a baking sheet in cooking spray.
> In a large mixing bowl add all of the ingredients. Toss until well combined. Spread the carrots out on the baking sheet and bake 40 – 45 minutes, or until lightly browned.

GREEK POTATOES

Servings: 6

Prep Time: Under 5 mins

Cooking Time: 1 hr 30 mins

(Per Serving)

Calories: 212

Protein: 3 grams

Carbohydrates: 40 grams

Fat: 5 grams

4 large potatoes, peeled and cut into large wedges

2 garlic cloves, minced

2 tablespoons extra-virgin olive oil

1 cup water

1 tablespoon dried oregano

1 lemon, juiced

1/2 teaspoon salt

1/4 teaspoon ground black pepper

> Preheat oven to 420°F/220 °C/Gas mark 7. Coat a baking dish in cooking spray.

> Place all of the ingredients in the baking dish and toss until well combined.

> Place in oven and bake for 40 minutes, or until a nice golden-brown crust has formed on the potatoes. Remove from oven and stir to bring the white underside up, sprinkle with a little more salt, pepper, and oregano.

> If the dish is getting dry add another 1/2 cup of water and place back in oven for another 40 minutes, or until new top is browned.

CREAMY CAULIFLOWER MASH

Servings: 8

Prep Time: 5 mins

Cooking Time: 20 – 25 mins

(Per Serving)

Calories: 231

Protein: 7 grams

Carbohydrates: 34 grams

Fat: 8 grams

3 cups cauliflower florets, steamed and chopped

1/2 cup cashews, soaked and drained

1/4 cup water

1 lemon, juiced

1/4 teaspoon salt

1 1/2 cups millet, cooked (available in Tescos)

> In a food processor or blender, add the cashews, water, lemon juice, and salt and process until smooth. Add the cauliflower and continue to process until well combined.

> Slowly add in the millet and process until desired consistency (I like mine with a little texture).

SPICED RED CABBAGE

Servings: 6

Prep Time: Under 5 mins

Cooking Time: 1 hr

(Per Serving)

Calories: 63

Protein: 2 grams

Carbohydrates: 11 grams

Fat: 3 grams

1/2 medium head red cabbage, diced

1 tablespoon canola/vegetable oil

1/2 cup onion, chopped

1 medium apple, quartered

3 tablespoons tarragon vinegar

1 teaspoon stevia or other natural sweetener

1 bay leaf

1 teaspoon salt

1/4 teaspoon ground black pepper

1/8 teaspoon ground cloves

> Add 1 inch/2 ½ cm of water to a large saucepan and place over medium-high heat. Add the cabbage and bring to a boil. Reduce heat, cover and simmer for 4 – 5 minutes, until crisp. Drain.

> Return to pan, add the remaining ingredients and mix well. Cover and simmer for 1 hour or until cabbage is tender. Remove bay leaf before serving.

CRANBERRY-APRICOT SQUASH/MARROW

Servings: 4

Prep Time: Under 5 mins

Cooking Time: Under 10 mins

(Per Serving)

Calories: 175

Protein: 2 grams

Carbohydrates: 32 grams

Fat: 6 grams

1 pound/450 grams delicata squash or marrow, seeded and chopped into bite-sized pieces

1 tablespoon extra-virgin olive oil

1 tablespoon apple cider

1/4 teaspoon salt

1/4 teaspoon ground black pepper

1/4 cup dried apricots, chopped

1/4 cup dried cranberries

2 tablespoons chives, finely chopped

2 tablespoons sliced almonds, toasted

> Preheat the oven to 375 °F/190 °C/Gas mark 5.

> Place a large saucepan with about 1 inch/2 ½ cm of water over medium-high heat and bring to a boil. Place the squash in a steamer basket and steam until tender, about 5 – 7 minutes.

> In a large mixing bowl, add the olive oil, apple cider, salt, and pepper and whisk until well combined. Add the squash, apricots, cranberries, and chives and toss to coat. Sprinkle with almonds.

QUINOA & SMOKED TOFU SALAD

Servings: 6

Prep Time: 10 mins

Cooking Time: 20 mins

Cooling Time: 10 – 15 mins

(Per Serving)

Calories: 206

Protein: 10 grams

Carbohydrates: 23 grams

Fat: 8 grams

1 cup quinoa, rinsed

2 cups water

3/4 teaspoon salt, divided

1/4 cup lemon juice

2 tablespoons extra-virgin olive oil

2 cloves garlic, minced

1/4 teaspoon ground black pepper

1 (6 ounce/170 grams) package baked smoked tofu, diced

1 yellow bell pepper, diced

1 cup cherry tomatoes, halved

1 cup cucumber, diced

1/2 cup fresh parsley, chopped

1/2 cup fresh mint, chopped

> Add the water and 1/2 teaspoon of salt to a medium saucepan and place over medium-high heat. Bring to a boil, add the quinoa and return to a boil. Reduce to low, cover and cook until water has been fully absorbed, about 15 – 20 minutes.

> Meanwhile, in a large mixing bowl, add the lemon juice, olive oil, garlic, pepper, and the remaining 1/4 teaspoon of salt. Whisk together until well combined.

> Spread the quinoa out on a baking sheet to cool for at least 10 minutes. Add the cooled quinoa, tofu, bell pepper, tomatoes, cucumber, parsley, and mint to the dressing. Toss until well coated.

PEAR & QUINOA SALAD

Servings: 6

Prep Time: Under 5 mins

Cooking Time: 15 – 20 mins

(Per Serving)

Calories: 231

Protein: 7 grams

Carbohydrates: 34 grams

Fat: 8 grams

14 ounces/400 grams low-sodium vegetable broth

1 cup quinoa, rinsed

2 tablespoons canola/vegetable oil

1 tablespoon pear or raspberry vinegar

1/4 cup fresh chives, diced

1/4 teaspoon salt

1/4 teaspoon ground black pepper

2 medium pears, diced

1/8 cup walnuts, chopped

> Add the vegetable broth to a large saucepan and place over medium-high heat. Once boiling, add the quinoa and reduce heat to medium low to simmer. Stir well and cover with a tight fitting lid. Cook for about 15 minutes, until all the liquid is absorbed.

> Meanwhile, in a large mixing bowl add the oil, vinegar, chives, salt, and pepper and whisk to combine. Add the pears and toss to coat.

> Pour the cooked quinoa into the mixing bowl and mix until well combined. Sprinkle nuts over top. Can be served chilled or warm.

SNACKS

MEETING YOUR DAILY CALORIC and nutritional requirements is going to mean eating "snack" meals in between your breakfasts, lunches, and dinners. You might have to change your definition of "snack," however.

When I say "snack," I don't mean crackers, cookies, muffins, cereal, doughnuts, chips, pretzels, ice cream, cheese, candy, or any other tempting little late-night nibbles. If you have any of these nutritionally bankrupt foods in your home, I recommend you throw them out right now. Yes, all of them, because at best they're "empty" calories and at worst, actually harmful to your muscle-building or fat-loss ambitions.

Instead, you should stock up on healthy snacks such as low-fat cottage cheese, fresh fruits and vegetables, low-fat or fat-free yogurt, nuts, and granola.

What about protein bars for snacks? Most protein bars sold in stores are better snacks than Snickers bars, but that's not saying much.

The problem with most protein bars is they contain a large amount of junk carbs such as sugar and high fructose corn syrup, and not much protein (and to make matters even worse, some companies selling these bars claim they have more protein than they do!). Most bars also contain artificial sweeteners such as sucralose or aspartame, chemicals to enhance the taste, and chemical preservatives. There's just too much junk in most to make them worth eating.

In this section of the book, I'm going to show you how to make your own delicious protein bars using healthy, high-quality ingredients, along with a few other yummy snacks.

SNACK RECIPES FOR VEGETARIANS

MAPLE PUMPKIN PROTEIN BARS

Servings: 10 (1 bar per serving)

Prep Time: Under 5 mins

Cooking Time: 15 – 18 mins

(Per Serving)

Calories: 252

Protein: 20 grams

Carbohydrates: 38 grams

Fat: 2 grams

1 (15 ounce/425 grams) can Lima beans, drained and rinsed

1/2 cup pumpkin purée (available in Waitrose/Tescos)

4 tablespoons maple syrup

1 teaspoon pumpkin pie spice/allspice

1/4 teaspoon salt

1 cup raisin bran cereal

6 scoops vanilla whey protein powder (available in Tescos and Holland & Barratt)

1 1/2 cups old-fashioned oats

1 cup spelt flour

> Preheat oven to 350°F/180 °C/Gas mark 4.

> In a food processor or blender add all the ingredients except the oats and flour. Blend until smooth, then pour in dry ingredients and pulse until just combined.

> Lightly coat a 9 x 13 inch/ 23 x 33 cm baking dish in cooking spray and spread the mixture out evenly.

> Place in oven and bake for 15 – 18 minutes, or until set. Remove and cut into 10 bars.

MEXICAN BEAN DIP

Servings: 12 (2 tbsps per serving)

Prep Time: 5 mins

Cooking Time: Under 5 mins

(Per Serving)

Calories: 47

Protein: 3 grams

Carbohydrates: 6 grams

Fat: 1 gram

1/2 cup scallions/spring onions, thinly sliced

1 clove garlic, minced

1 can (15 ounce/425 grams) black beans, drained and rinsed

3/4 cup low-fat cheddar cheese, shredded

1/4 teaspoon salt

1/3 cup low-sodium vegetable broth

2 tablespoons coriander, finely chopped

> Coat a small skillet in cooking spray and place over medium heat. Add the spring onions and sauté until tender, about 3 minutes.

> In a food processor or blender, add the beans, cheddar cheese, and salt and blend for 5 seconds. Slowly add in the broth and continue to blend until desired dipping consistency. Transfer to large bowl and mix in the scallions and cilantro/coriander.

MEXI MELT

Servings: 1

Prep Time: Under 5 mins

Cooking Time: Under 5 mins

(Per Serving)

Calories: 139

Protein: 7 grams

Carbohydrates: 22 grams

Fat: 3 grams

2 tablespoons canned fat-free refried beans

1 slice whole grain bread, toasted

1 tablespoon salsa

1 tablespoon Jack/mature cheddar cheese, shredded

> Spread the beans out on the toast, top with salsa and sprinkle with cheese. Place in toaster oven or microwave on high until cheese is melted and beans are hot.

PROTEIN PARFAIT

Servings: 1

Prep Time: Under 5 mins

(Per Serving)

Calories: 225

Protein: 26 grams

Carbohydrates: 31 grams

Fat: 1 gram

1 cup fat-free plain Greek yogurt

1 cup pineapple or comparable fruit, diced

2 teaspoons toasted wheat germ

> Place the yogurt in a small bowl, top with fruit and sprinkle on wheat germ.

EASY FROSTED GRAPES

Servings: 4

Prep Time: Under 5 mins

(Per Serving)

Calories: 80

Protein: 1 gram

Carbohydrates: 21 grams

Fat: 0 gram

2 cups seedless grapes, washed and patted dry

1 cup fat-free whipped topping (Instant Whip or Angel Delight)

> Add the grapes to a large bowl and place in the freezer for at least 1 hour.
> Divide into 4 portions, top each with 1/4 cup of the whipped topping.

SNACK RECIPES FOR VEGANS

BLUEBERRY BANANA OAT CAKES

Servings: 4 (1 cake per serving)

Prep Time: Under 5 mins

Cooking Time: 3 – 5 mins

(Per Serving)

Calories: 95

Protein: 2 grams

Carbohydrates: 20 grams

Fat: 1 gram

1/2 cup old-fashioned oats

1 banana, mashed

2 tablespoons brown sugar

1 teaspoon cinnamon

1/4 cup fresh or frozen blueberries

> Pour all ingredients except blueberries into a medium-sized mixing bowl. Gently fold in the blueberries.
> Coat a shallow microwave-safe dish in cooking spray and pour the batter in.
> Microwave for 3 – 5 minutes (depending on the power of your microwave). Let cool for a few minutes before removing from dish, then cut into quarters.

CHOCOLATE BLACK BEAN ENERGY BARS

Servings: 10 (1 bar per serving)

Prep Time: Under 5 mins

Cooking Time: 15 – 20 mins

(Per Serving)

Calories: 306

Protein: 8 grams

Carbohydrates: 50 grams

Fat: 12 grams

1 1/2 cups black beans, rinsed

1/2 cup almond butter (available in Asda)

1/4 cup agave nectar (available in Waitrose and Holland & Barratt)

1/4 cup banana, mashed

1 teaspoon vanilla extract

1/4 teaspoon salt

1/2 cup cocoa powder

1/2 cup coconut, shredded

1/2 cup raisins

1 1/2 cups old-fashioned oats

1/2 cup brown rice flour (available in Asda and Holland & Barratt)

> Preheat oven to 350°F/180 °C/Gas mark 4.

> In a food processor or blender add all the ingredients except the oats and flour. Blend until smooth, then pour in dry ingredients and pulse until just combined.

> Lightly coat a 9 x 13 inch/23 x 33 cm baking dish in cooking spray and spread the mixture out evenly.

> Place in oven and bake for 15 – 18 minutes, or until set. Remove and cut into 10 bars.

BAKED KALE CHIPS

Servings: 1

Prep Time: Under 5 mins

Cooking Time: 20 mins

(Per Serving)

Calories: 34

Protein: 2 grams

Carbohydrates: 7 grams

Fat: 1 gram

1 cup kale, chopped

salt, to taste

> Preheat oven to 300°F/150 °C/Gas mark 2. Coat a baking sheet in cooking spray.
> Rinse and dry the kale. Cut off the stems and tough centre ribs, and then chop into bite-sized pieces. Place on the baking sheet and apply a layer of cooking spray and salt on top of the kale.
> Place in oven and bake for 20 minutes or until crisp. Let cool before eating.

SEASONED PITTA CHIPS

Servings: 6 (6 chips per serving)

Prep Time: Under 5 mins

Cooking Time: 5 – 10 mins

(Per Serving)

Calories: 80

Protein: 3 grams

Carbohydrates: 15 grams

Fat: 1 gram

3 whole grain pittas

3 tablespoons Italian seasoning

1 teaspoon chilli powder

1 teaspoon garlic powder

1 teaspoon salt

> Preheat oven to 425°F/220 °C/Gas mark 7. Coat a baking sheet in cooking spray.

> Cut pittas in half, stack all 6 halves and cut into 6 wedges. Spread the wedges out soft side up on the baking sheet. Sprinkle with spices and a light coat of cooking spray.

> Place in oven and bake 5 – 10 minutes, until browned and crisp.

VEGETABLE HUMMUS

Servings: 12 (2 tbsps per serving)

Prep Time: Under 5 mins

(Per Serving)

Calories: 79

Protein: 2 grams

Carbohydrates: 9 grams

Fat: 4 grams

1/3 cup carrots, shredded

1/3 cup fresh parsley

1/4 cup scallions/spring onions, sliced

1 1/2 cups cooked chickpeas (if canned, drained)

1/4 cup tahini

3 tablespoons lemon juice

2 tablespoons extra-virgin olive oil

2 cloves garlic, minced

1/4 teaspoon salt

1/8 teaspoon ground black pepper

> In a food processor or blender, add the carrots, parsley, and scallions and process until finely chopped.

> Add the remaining ingredients and process until smooth or desired consistency.

LEMON CASHEW HEMP BARS

Servings: 8 (1 bar per serving)

Prep Time: Under 5 mins

Chilling Time: 30 – 40 mins

(Per Serving)

Calories: 249

Protein: 16 grams

Carbohydrates: 23 grams

Fat: 12 grams

1 cup cashews

1 cup pitted dates

1/3 cup hemp seeds (available in Holland & Barratt)

1 cup hemp protein powder (available in Holland & Barratt)

2 tablespoons lemon juice

1 tablespoon lemon zest

> Place the cashews in a food processor or blender and process until ground.

> Add the dates, hemp seeds, and hemp protein and pulse until well combined. Add the lemon juice and lemon zest and process until sticky.

> Place a layer of plastic wrap down on a small baking dish. Spread out the mixture evenly over top of the plastic wrap, and then cover with another layer of plastic wrap.

> Place in freezer for at least 30 minutes. Remove and cut into 8 bars.

BANANA PROTEIN FLUFF

Servings: 1

Prep Time: 1 hr, including freezing

(Per Serving)

Calories: 245

Protein: 24 grams

Carbohydrates: 32 grams

Fat: 2 grams

1 banana, sliced

1 tablespoon coconut extract (available in Holland & Barratt)

1/2 cup almond milk (available in Tescos and Holland & Barratt)

2 scoops chocolate brown rice protein (available in Asda and Holland & Barratt)

dash of cinnamon

> Place the banana and coconut extract into a ziplock bag, shake until well combined and place in the freezer.
> Once frozen, place the banana and almond milk in a blender and blend until it forms a mush.
> Transfer mixture to a medium-sized mixing bowl; add the protein powder and blend with an electric mixer for 5 minutes, or until it becomes fluffy. Top with a dash of cinnamon.

ZUCCHINI/ COURGETTE HUMMUS ROLLS

Servings: 1 (2 rolls per serving)

Prep Time: 10 mins

(Per Serving)

Calories: 129

Protein: 4 grams

Carbohydrates: 16 grams

Fat: 5 grams

6 thin strips zucchini/courgette

2 slices tomato, halved

4 tablespoons hummus

> Using a potato peeler or julienne peeler cut out 6 thin strips of zucchini/ courgette.
> Lay out 3 pieces, slightly overlapping. Top with 2 tablespoons hummus, then 2 halves of tomato. Roll up lengthwise. Repeat.

HOMEMADE APPLE SAUCE

Servings: 4

Prep Time: Under 5 mins

Cooking Time: 15 – 20 mins

(Per Serving)

Calories: 95

Protein: 1 gram

Carbohydrates: 25 grams

Fat: 0 grams

4 apples, peeled, cored, and chopped

3/4 cup water

1 teaspoon stevia or other natural sweetener

1/2 teaspoon ground cinnamon

> Place a large saucepan over medium heat. Add all of the ingredients. Mix well, then cover and let cook for 15 – 20 minutes, or until the apples have become soft.

> Allow to cool, then blend or mash until desired consistency.

CUCUMBER SALAD

Servings: 4

Prep Time: 5 – 10 mins

Cooking Time: 2 – 3 mins

Chilling Time: 1 hr

(Per Serving)

Calories: 44

Protein: 2 grams

Carbohydrates: 8 grams

Fat: 0 grams

4 cucumbers, thinly sliced

1 small white onion, thinly sliced

1/4 teaspoon salt

1/4 teaspoon ground black pepper

1 cup white vinegar

1/2 cup water

1 teaspoon stevia or other natural sweetener

1 tablespoon dried dill

> In a large mixing bowl, add the cucumbers, onions, salt, and pepper and toss until well combined.

> Place a small saucepan over medium heat. Add the vinegar, water, and stevia. Bring to a boil, then pour over the cucumber mixture. Stir in the dill, cover and refrigerate until chilled, at least 1 hour.

NO-BAKE ALMOND PROTEIN BARS

Servings: 10

Prep Time: 10 mins

Cooking Time: 10 mins

(Per Serving)

Calories: 218

Protein: 13 grams

Carbohydrates: 23 grams

Fat: 8 grams

1 cup old-fashioned oats

1 cup brown rice cereal (available in Asda and Holland & Barratt)

1 cup hemp protein powder (available in Holland & Barratt)

1/2 teaspoon ground cinnamon

1 teaspoon salt

1/2 cup brown rice syrup (available in Asda and Holland & Barratt)

1/2 cup almond butter (available in Asda)

2 tablespoons vanilla extract

> In a large mixing bowl, add the oats, cereal, protein powder, cinnamon, and salt. Mix until well combined.

> In a medium-sized microwave-safe bowl, add the brown rice syrup and almond butter. Microwave for 45 seconds to soften, and then stir in the vanilla extract.

> Pour the wet mixture over the dry and mix until well combined. I recommend using your (slightly wet) hands for this.

> Lightly coat a baking dish in cooking spray, pour the batter into the pan. Again, I recommend using slightly wet fingers to evenly spread the batter out over the dish.

> Place in the freezer for 10 minutes, or until set. Remove and cut into 10 bars. Keep covered and store in fridge or freezer.

ITALIAN VEGGIE ANTIPASTO

Servings: 6

Prep Time: 5 mins

Cooking Time: 5 – 10 mins

Chilling Time: 30 – 40

(Per Serving)

Calories: 58

Protein: 3 grams

Carbohydrates: 9 grams

Fat: 2 grams

2 cups white vinegar

2 cups water

1 teaspoon stevia or other natural sweetener

1 bay leaf

1 teaspoon red pepper flakes, divided

1 teaspoon salt, divided

1 medium head cauliflower, trimmed and cut into florets

2 stalks celery, thinly sliced

1 carrot, thinly sliced

1 red bell pepper, sliced

1 tablespoon extra-virgin olive oil

1/4 teaspoon ground black pepper

> Place a large saucepan over medium-high heat. Add the vinegar, water, stevia, bay leaf, and 1/2 teaspoon each of the red pepper flakes and salt. Bring to a boil.

> Add the cauliflower, celery, carrot, and bell pepper and mix well. Reduce heat to medium and simmer for about 5 minutes, or until vegetables are tender. Remove from heat and let sit for 5 minutes.

> Save 3 tablespoons of the cooking liquid and drain the rest. Transfer the vegetables to a large mixing bowl. Add the oil, pepper, reserved cooking liquid, and the remaining 1/2 teaspoons of red pepper flakes and salt. Toss until well combined.

> Cover and refrigerate for at least 30 minutes, serve chilled.

3 FAST & SIMPLE EGG SALAD RECIPES

Egg salad is a great fast food because it's high in protein, low in fat, and can be quickly prepared in many ways. Each of these recipes can be prepared in around 15 minutes.

Below are three different ways to make quick and tasty egg salad snacks.

VEGETARIAN:

SWEET SOUTHERN EGG SALAD

Servings: 4

Prep Time: 5 mins

Cooking Time: 7 – 8 mins

(Per Serving)

Calories: 137

Protein: 13 grams

Carbohydrates: 10 grams

Fat: 5 grams

3 tablespoons fat-free Greek yogurt

3 tablespoons low-fat mayonnaise

2 teaspoons mustard

1/4 teaspoon ground black pepper

1/8 teaspoon salt

12 hard-boiled eggs

1/2 cup thinly sliced celery

1/4 cup chopped sweet pickles

> In a medium-sized mixing bowl, add the yogurt, mayonnaise, mustard, pepper, and salt. Mix until well combined.

> Remove all of the egg yolks, save 2 and discard the rest, add the egg whites and the remaining yolks to the mixing bowl and mash until desired consistency. Add the celery, pickles, and onions and mix.

VEGETABLE EGG SALAD

Servings: 4

Prep Time: 5 – 10 mins

Cooking Time: 7 – 8 mins

(Per Serving)

Calories: 130

Protein: 13 grams

Carbohydrates: 8 grams

Fat: 5 grams

3 tablespoons fat-free Greek yogurt

3 tablespoons low-fat mayonnaise

1/4 teaspoon ground black pepper

1/8 teaspoon salt

12 hard-boiled eggs

1/2 cup finely chopped carrots

1/2 cup chopped cucumber

1/4 cup chopped scallions/spring onions

> In a medium-sized mixing bowl, add the yogurt, mayonnaise, pepper, and salt. Mix until well combined.

> Remove all of the egg yolks, save 2 and discard the rest, add the egg whites and the remaining yolks to the mixing bowl and mash until desired consistency. Add the carrots, cucumbers, and scallions and mix.

VEGAN:
EGGLESS EGG SALAD

Servings: 4

Prep Time: 10 mins

Cooking Time: At least 2 hrs

(Per Serving)

Calories: 108

Protein: 10 grams

Carbohydrates: 3 grams

Fat: 7 grams

2 tablespoons Vegenaise (try Plamil, available from most major supermarkets)

1 tablespoon sweet relish

1 teaspoon distilled white vinegar

1 teaspoon mustard

1/4 teaspoon stevia or other natural sweetener

1/2 teaspoon ground turmeric

1/4 teaspoon dried dill

1 tablespoon dried parsley

1/8 teaspoon salt

1/4 teaspoon ground black pepper

1 pound drained and crumbled low-fat extra-firm tofu

1 tablespoon chopped onion

2 tablespoons chopped celery

> In a medium-sized mixing bowl, add the Vegenaise, relish, vinegar, mustard, stevia, turmeric, dill, parsley, salt, and pepper and mix well.

> In a separate bowl, add the tofu, onion, and celery and toss to combine. Pour the tofu mixture into the Vegenaise mixture and mix until well combined. Refrigerate for at least 2 hours before serving to let flavours combine.

PROTEIN SHAKES

PROTEIN SHAKES ARE A great way to help meet daily nutritional requirements, and are especially good for your post-workout meal due to
fast absorption of the protein and high-glycemic carbs.

I recommend that you use a high-quality whey (I like Optimum Nutrition's Natural Whey) or egg (I like Healthy 'N Fit's 100% Egg Protein
Powder) protein powder because both taste pretty good and have no artificial sweeteners.

For vegans, I recommend a good raw protein powder (I like the Gar-
den of Life raw protein products best). Brown rice protein is also a good
source (I like NutriBiotics' Organic Rice Protein), as well as hemp protein (I like the Living Harvest Tempt Hemp High Protein Formula) and
even pea protein.

If you're going to be making several shakes per day (as most of us
do), I recommend that you simply mix the powder with water and then
get your carbs from fruit or other sources. The shake recipes given in
this section require a blender and other ingredients, and are more suited
for your post-workout meals (these contain a lot of carbs), or as a meal
replacement.

Any shakes that contain whey protein can be replaced with a comparable amount of any vegan friendly protein.

PROTEIN SHAKE RECIPES
FOR VEGETARIANS

SIMPLE CHOCOLATE PROTEIN SHAKE

Servings: 1

Prep Time: Under 5 mins

(Per Serving)

Calories: 447

Protein: 33 grams

Carbohydrates: 44 grams

Fat: 18 grams

1 cup almond milk (available in Tesco and other major supermarkets)

1 banana

1 tablespoon sweetened cocoa

2 tablespoons cashews

1 scoop chocolate whey protein powder (available in Tesco and Holland & Barratt)

> Blend all ingredients together until desired consistency.

BLUEBERRY FLAX SMOOTHIE

Servings: 1

Prep Time: Under 5 mins

(Per Serving)

Calories: 481

Protein: 46 grams

Carbohydrates: 63 grams

Fat: 8 grams

1 1/4 cups plain fat-free Greek yogurt

1 cup frozen blueberries

1 banana

2 tablespoons ground flax seed (available in Holland & Barratt)

1/2 scoop vanilla whey protein powder (available in Holland & Barratt)

> Blend all ingredients together until desired consistency.

PEAR ALMOND SMOOTHIE

Servings: 1

Prep Time: Under 5 mins

(Per Serving)

Calories: 546

Protein: 23 grams

Carbohydrates: 79 grams

Fat: 15 grams

1 cup rice milk

1 banana, frozen

1/2 medium-sized pear

1/4 cup almonds

1/2 scoop chocolate whey protein powder (available in Holland & Barratt or Tesco)

> Blend all ingredients together until desired consistency.

CHERRY VANILLA PROTEIN SMOOTHIE

Servings: 1

Prep Time: Under 5 mins

(Per Serving)

Calories: 247

Protein: 27 grams

Carbohydrates: 29 grams

Fat: 4 grams

1 cup frozen cherries, without pits

1 scoop vanilla whey protein powder (available in Tesco and Holland and Barratt)

1 cup baby spinach

1 1/4 cups almond milk

4 – 6 ice cubes (optional)

> Blend all ingredients together until desired consistency.

THE KIWI

Servings: 1

Prep Time: Under 5 mins

(Per Serving)

Calories: 332

Protein: 29 grams

Carbohydrates: 47 grams

Fat: 4 grams

1 cup rice milk (available in major supermarkets)

2 tablespoons fat-free Greek yogurt

1 medium kiwi, peeled

1/2 cup strawberries

1 scoop vanilla whey protein powder (available in Tesco and Holland & Barratt)

3 – 4 ice cubes (optional)

> Blend all ingredients together until desired consistency.

DOUBLE CHOCOLATE PROTEIN SMOOTHIE

Servings: 1

Prep Time: Under 5 mins

(Per Serving)

Calories: 433

Protein: 36 grams

Carbohydrates: 52 grams

Fat: 10 grams

1 cup low-fat chocolate milk

2 tablespoons low-fat vanilla yogurt

1 tablespoon frozen orange juice concentrate

1/2 banana

1 tablespoon sliced almonds

1 scoop chocolate whey protein powder (available in Tesco and Holland & Barratt)

2 teaspoons ground flax seed (available in Holland & Barratt)

4 – 6 ice cubes (optional)

> Blend all ingredients together until desired consistency.

PUMPKIN DELIGHT

Servings: 1

Prep Time: Under 5 mins

(Per Serving)

Calories: 345

Protein: 36 grams

Carbohydrates: 36 grams

Fat: 4 grams

1/4 cup low-fat pecan frozen yogurt or hazelnut yogurt

1/2 cup canned pumpkin (available in most major supermarkets)

1 cup skimmed milk

1 scoop vanilla whey protein powder (available in Tesco or Holland & Barratt)

1 teaspoon ground flax seed (available in Holland & Barratt)

> Blend all ingredients together until desired consistency.

PROTEIN SHAKE RECIPES FOR VEGANS

BLACK & BLUEBERRY PROTEIN SMOOTHIE

Servings: 1

Prep Time: Under 5 mins

(Per Serving)

Calories: 412

Protein: 28 grams

Carbohydrates: 58 grams

Fat: 10 grams

1 banana, frozen

1/2 cup blueberries

1/2 cup blackberries

1 cup almond milk (available in Tesco and Holland & Barratt)

1 tablespoon cacao nibs (available online with Amazon)

1 serving hemp protein powder (available in Holland & Barratt)

4 – 6 ice cubes (optional)

> Blend all ingredients together until desired consistency.

MANGO-LIME HOT PEPPER SMOOTHIE

Servings: 1

Prep Time: Under 5 mins

(Per Serving)

Calories: 467

Protein: 26 grams

Carbohydrates: 85 grams

Fat: 7 grams

1 lime, juiced

1 banana

1 mango, peeled and pitted

1/2 jalapeño

1 1/2 cups water

1 cup ice

1 tablespoon ground flax seed (available in Holland & Barratt)

1 serving hemp protein powder (available in Holland & Barratt)

1 tablespoon agave nectar (available in major supermarkets)

> Blend all ingredients together until desired consistency.

CHERRY CINNAMON PROTEIN BLAST

Servings: 1

Prep Time: Under 5 mins

(Per Serving)

Calories: 282

Protein: 27 grams

Carbohydrates: 38 grams

Fat: 3 grams

1/2 large banana, frozen

3/4 cup pitted cherries

2 teaspoons cinnamon

1 cup almond milk (available in Tesco and Holland & Barratt)

2 tablespoons rice protein powder (available in Holland & Barratt)

4 – 6 ice cubes (optional)

> Blend all ingredients together until desired consistency.

DESSERTS

DON'T WORRY—I HAVEN'T forgotten the sweets. Don't think of your hard training as a license to indulge in treats regularly, though. You can kill your fat loss pretty quickly by simply adding a couple hundred calories too many each day.

That being said, there's nothing wrong with having a dessert every week or two. When I'm eating to gain muscle, I usually have one dessert per week (although some weeks I skip it—I'm not really into sugar). When I'm dieting to lose weight, I never have more than one small dessert per week, and I usually have one every two weeks.

The recipes I give here are better than your average dessert recipes in that they have no sugar and little fat. They use higher-quality carbs than your average junk at the store, and they are high in protein, which puts them lower on the glycemic index.

DESSERT RECIPES FOR VEGETARIANS

PROTEIN PEACH SURPRISE

Servings: 1

Prep Time: Under 5 mins

Cooking Time: 8 – 10 mins

(Per Serving)

Calories: 182

Protein: 22 grams

Carbohydrates: 21 grams

Fat: 2 grams

1 cup peaches

1/4 cup fat-free cream cheese

1/4 teaspoon cinnamon

1/2 scoop vanilla whey protein powder (available in Tesco and Holland & Barratt)

> Preheat oven to 500°F/260 °C/Gas mark 10.
> In a small bowl mix together the cream cheese, cinnamon, and protein powder. Place the peaches on a baking sheet, bake for 8 – 10 minutes.
> Top cream cheese mixture with baked peaches.

RECOVERY RICE KRISPIES

Servings: 8 (1 piece per serving)

Prep Time: Under 5 mins

Cooking Time: 10 – 15 mins

(Per Serving)

Calories: 80

Protein: 4 grams

Carbohydrates: 10 grams

Fat: 3 grams

1 1/2 cups Rice Krispies

2 tablespoons unsalted butter

1 1/2 tablespoons honey

1/2 teaspoon vanilla extract

1 scoop vanilla whey protein powder (available in Tesco and Holland & Barratt)

1/2 cup old-fashioned oats

> Preheat oven to 325°F/160 °C/Gas mark 3. Coat a 9 x 9 inch/23 x 23 cm baking dish in cooking spray.

> In a small saucepan over medium-low heat, melt the butter, honey, and vanilla extract until smooth. Add the protein powder and continue to stir until it forms a thick substance. Remove from heat.

> Stir in the Rice Krispies and oats, and then transfer to the baking dish. Press down with a fork and bake 10 – 15 minutes, or until crisp. Once cool, cut into 8 pieces.

NO-BAKE VANILLA CAKE

Servings: 1

Prep Time: Under mins

Cooking Time: 2 mins, or until set

(Per Serving)

Calories: 344

Protein: 18 grams

Carbohydrates: 62 grams

Fat: 2 grams

1 egg

3 tablespoons unsweetened apple sauce

2 tablespoons vanilla or maple syrup

3 tablespoons skimmed milk

1/2 teaspoon vanilla extract

2 tablespoons whole grain flour

3 tablespoons pancake mix

1/2 scoop vanilla whey protein powder (available in Tesco or Holland & Barratt)

> In a blender, add the egg, apple sauce, syrup, skimmed milk, and vanilla extract and blend until well combined and smooth.

> One at a time pour in the flour, pancake mix, and protein powder and blend until well combined.

> Transfer the cake mix to a microwave-safe bowl and microwave on high for 2 minutes (if the top is still not fully set microwave for an additional 10 seconds at a time until set).

BLACKBERRY PARFAIT

Servings: 1

Prep Time: Under 5 mins

(Per Serving)

Calories: 279

Protein: 23 grams

Carbohydrates: 47 grams

Fat: 2 grams

6 ounces/170 grams fat-free Greek yogurt

2 teaspoons honey

1/4 cup granola

1/2 cup blackberries

1/4 cup nectarine, chopped

> Mix honey into yogurt. In a small bowl or cup, add the granola, then the yogurt. Top with fruit.

RICE PUDDING

Servings: 4

Prep Time: Under 5 mins

Cooking Time: 20 – 25 mins

(Per Serving)

Calories: 191

Protein: 8 grams

Carbohydrates: 37 grams

Fat: 0 grams

3 cups skimmed milk

1/2 cup Arborio rice

1/3 cup raisins

1/2 teaspoon stevia or other natural sweetener

2 teaspoons lemon zest

1 teaspoon vanilla extract

1/8 teaspoon salt

1/4 teaspoon cinnamon

> In a medium saucepan, add the milk, rice, raisins, and stevia and place over medium-high heat. Bring to a boil, stirring constantly. Reduce heat to low and simmer, stirring frequently, until the rice is tender,

about 20 – 25 minutes. Stir constantly toward the end to prevent burning.

> Remove from heat, add the lemon zest, vanilla extract, and salt and mix well. Sprinkle with cinnamon.

RUM BANANAS

Servings: 2

Prep Time: Under 5 mins

Cooking Time: 5 – 10 mins

(Per Serving)

Calories: 201

Protein: 2 grams

Carbohydrates: 34 grams

Fat: 5 grams

2 bananas, quartered

2 tablespoons brown sugar

1 teaspoon butter

1/2 teaspoon canola/vegetable oil

2 tablespoons dark rum

1 teaspoon lime juice

1/8 teaspoon cinnamon

4 tablespoons vanilla Greek yogurt

> Place a medium-sized non-stick skillet over medium heat. Add the brown sugar, butter, and oil, and sauté until bubbling.

> Add the rum, lime juice, and cinnamon and continue to sauté until slightly thickened.

> Add the bananas, cook, stirring occasionally, until tender. Divide into 2 equal portions and top with 2 tablespoons vanilla yogurt.

DESSERT RECIPES FOR VEGANS

BANANA CARAMEL BREAD PUDDING

Servings: 4

Prep Time: 10 mins

Cooking Time: 30 mins

(Per Serving)

Calories: 407

Protein: 9 grams

Carbohydrates: 83 grams

Fat: 10 grams

2 large bananas, ripe

1/2 cup dates

3/4 cup almond milk

2 teaspoons cinnamon

8 slices whole grain cinnamon raisin bread, cubed

1/2 cup coconut milk

> Preheat oven to 375°F/190 °C/Gas mark 5.
> In a food processor or liquidiser, blitz the dates until as smooth as possible.
> Add the bananas, almond milk, and cinnamon and blend until smooth.
> Transfer to a large mixing bowl. Add the bread cubes to the mixing bowl and mix until well combined.

> Divide the bread mixture into 4 ramekins; pour 2 tablespoons of the coconut milk over each. Place in oven and bake for 30 minutes, or until bread is golden and caramelized.

ROASTED PINEAPPLE

Servings: 2 (3 slices per servings)

Prep Time: Under 5 mins

Cooking Time: 20 – 25 mins

(Per Serving)

Calories: 117

Protein: 1 gram

Carbohydrates: 31 grams

Fat: 0 grams

6 slices pineapple, about 1/2-inch-1 ½ cm thick

2 tablespoons brown sugar

> Preheat grill. Coat a baking sheet in cooking spray.
> Spread out the pineapple on the baking sheet and sprinkle with brown sugar. Grill for 10 – 15 minutes, or until golden brown. Flip and grill for another 5 – 10 minutes, until golden brown.

CHOCOLATE SWEET POTATO PUDDING

Servings: 2

Prep Time: Under 5 mins

(Per Serving)

Calories: 253

Protein: 4 grams

Carbohydrates: 37 grams

Fat: 13 grams

1/2 medium sweet potato, cooked

1 medium avocado

5 dates, pitted and soaked

2 tablespoons carob or chocolate powder

1/4 cup water

> In a food processor or blender add all of the ingredients and pulse until ingredients are mostly mixed. Turn on high and slowly add any additional water until the pudding is smooth.

CRAN-STRAWBERRY POPSICLES

Servings: 8

Prep Time: Under 5 mins

Cooking Time: 1 hr, or until set

(Per Serving)

Calories: 31

Protein: 0 grams

Carbohydrates: 8 grams

Fat: 0 grams

2 cups fresh strawberries

1/4 cup frozen cranberry juice concentrate, thawed (available in Tescos)

1 teaspoon stevia or other natural sweetener

1 tablespoon lemon juice

3 tablespoons water

> In a blender or food processor, add the strawberries, cranberry concentrate, stevia, lemon juice, and water and process until smooth.
> Pour the mixture into 8 popsicle moulds or small paper cups. Place in freezer until they begin to set, about 1 hour. Insert popsicle sticks and place back in freezer until completely set.

BONUS SPREADSHEET

First, I want to say THANK YOU for reading my book,
Eat Green, Get Lean.

I'm thrilled at how many people have written me to say how much they like the recipes for helping with losing weight, building muscle, and staying healthy.

Chances are you'd like to use the recipes in this book to plan out your daily meals. This handy spreadsheet will help!

In it you'll find a list of every recipe in the book along with their calories, protein, carbs, and fats. When you're planning your meals, all you have to do is skim over the spreadsheet and pick foods that fit your caloric and macronutritional targets. No need to browse through the entire cookbook!

Visit the link below to download this free spreadsheet today!

Visit .BIT.LY/LEANGREEN-BONUS to get this spread-sheet now!

WOULD YOU DO ME A FAVOR?

Thank you for buying my book. I hope that you enjoy the recipes I've included and that they help you in your muscle-building and fat-torching endeavors.

I have a small favor to ask. Would you mind taking a minute to write a blurb on Amazon about this book? I check all my reviews and love to get feedback (that's the real pay for my work—knowing that I'm helping people).

Visit the following page to leave me a review:

WWW.AMZN.TO/LEANGREEN-REVIEW

Also, if you have any friends or family that might enjoy this book, spread the love and lend it to them!

Now, I don't just want to sell you a book—I want to see you use what you've learned to build the body of your dreams.

As you work toward your goals, however, you'll probably have questions or run into some difficulties. I'd like to be able to help you with these, so let's connect up! I don't charge for the help, of course, and I answer questions from readers every day.

Here's how we can connect:

Facebook: facebook.com/muscleforlifefitness

Twitter: @muscleforlife

G+: gplus.to/MuscleForLife

And last but not least, my website is www.muscleforlife.com and if you want to write me, my email address is mike@muscleforlife.com.

Thanks again and I wish you the best!

Mike

P.S. Turn to the next page to check out other books of mine that you might like!

ALSO BY MICHAEL MATTHEWS

Thinner Leaner Stronger: The Simple Science of Building the Ultimate Female Body

If you want to be toned, lean, and strong as quickly as possible without crash dieting, "good genetics," or wasting ridiculous amounts of time in the gym and money on supplements...regardless of your age...then you want to read this book.

Visit www.muscleforlife.com to get this book!

Bigger Leaner Stronger: The Simple Science of Building the Ultimate Male Body

If you want to be muscular, lean, and strong as quickly as possible, without steroids, good genetics, or wasting ridiculous amounts of time in the gym, and money on supplements...then you want to read this book.

Visit www.muscleforlife.com to get this book!

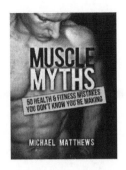

Muscle Myths: 50 Health & Fitness Mistakes You Don't Know You're Making

If you've ever felt lost in the sea of contradictory training and diet advice out there and you just want to know once and for all what works and what doesn't—what's scientifically true and what's false—when it comes to building muscle and getting ripped, then you need to read this book.

Visit www.muscleforlife.com to get this book!

Cardio Sucks! The Simple Science of Burning Fat Fast and Getting in Shape

If you're short on time and sick of the same old boring cardio routine and want to kick your fat loss into high gear by working out less and...heaven forbid...actually have some fun...then you want to read this new book.

Visit www.muscleforlife.com to get this book!

Awakening Your Inner Genius

If you'd like to know what some of history's greatest thinkers and achievers can teach you about awakening your inner genius, and how to find, follow, and fulfill your journey to greatness, then you want to read this book today.

(I'm using a pen name for this book, as well as for a few other projects not related to health and fitness, but I thought you might enjoy it so I'm including it here.)

Visit www.yourinnergenius.com to get this book!

The Shredded Chef: 120 Recipes for Building Muscle, Getting Lean, and Staying Healthy

If you want to know how to forever escape the dreadful experience of "dieting" and learn how to cook nutritious, delicious meals that make building muscle and burning fat easy and enjoyable, then you need to read this book.

Visit www.muscleforlife.com to get this book!

Printed in Great Britain
by Amazon.co.uk, Ltd.,
Marston Gate.